WHAT HAS COVID-19 TAUGHT US ABOUT ASIA'S HEALTH EMERGENCY PREPAREDNESS AND RESPONSE?

MARCH 2024

ASIAN DEVELOPMENT BANK

© 2024 Asian Development Bank
6 ADB Avenue, Mandaluyong City, 1550 Metro Manila, Philippines
Tel +63 2 8632 4444; Fax +63 2 8636 2444
www.adb.org

Some rights reserved. Published in 2024.

ISBN 978-92-9270-633-3 (print); 978-92-9270-634-0 (PDF); 978-92-9270-635-7 (ebook)
Publication Stock No. TCS240101-3
DOI: http://dx.doi.org/10.22617/TCS240101-3

Notes:
In this publication, "$" refers to United States dollars.
ADB recognizes "Hong Kong" as Hong Kong, China.

Cover design by Erickson Mercado.

CONTENTS

FOREWORD

The coronavirus disease (COVID-19) was an unprecedented health emergency. It was unique in how fast it spread. It caught governments off guard and rapidly overwhelmed health systems. Governments enacted sweeping lockdowns and social distancing measures, including school closures and work-from-home arrangements. Most continued for long periods as scientists scrambled to learn more about the virus, its contagion, mutation, and how to develop, test, and distribute vaccines. Their impact on society was dramatic. Life was disrupted. The global economy suffered. Education suffered. They allowed governments to buy time and forge support measures to keep people and firms going.

Once vaccines became widely available and mobility restrictions were lifted, the focus shifted to recovery. It was also time to begin acknowledging what worked and what did not. Four years after COVID-19 was declared a global pandemic, economies learned that some lockdown measures were too stringent and in place too long. It not only created immediate and lingering economic hardship, but also likely led to long-term scarring in terms of lost human capital. Some economies were able to apply more effective measures, minimizing both the short- and long-term effects on their citizens, providing important lessons. The pandemic also magnified the pre-existing gaps between high- and low-income economies, as well as between families with high versus low socioeconomic status within economies. For example, access to vaccines and other medical help was highly unequal in many places.

Learning from the responses to COVID-19 is critical. While no one can predict the type or timing of the next health emergency, another will undoubtably occur. Governments need to adequately prepare their health systems and capacity to respond to emergencies. This report makes recommendations on health emergency preparedness by reviewing the lessons learned from the COVID-19 pandemic experience. It highlights the need for better and more real-time data. It assesses the cost-effectiveness of both non-pharmaceutical and pharmaceutical interventions. While the report is necessarily limited in scope, it provides lessons and recommendations that will be useful for policymakers across Asia and the Pacific, and elsewhere.

ALBERT F. PARK
Chief Economist
Asian Development Bank

ACKNOWLEDGMENTS

This report was authored by Minhaj Mahmud, Arief Ramayandi, and Dennis Sorino, all from ADB's Economic Research and Development Impact Department (ERDI), and Daniel Suryadarma from the Asian Development Bank Institute. Abdul Abiad, director of the Macroeconomics Research Division, led the production of the report.

ERDI management, including ADB Chief Economist Albert Park, Deputy Chief Economist Joseph E. Zveglich Jr., and Director Lei Lei Song provided guidance, support, and feedback. Further input was also provided by Rhea Molato-Gayares from ERDI, Najibullah Habib, Vasoontara Yiengprugsawan, Dinesh Arora, Sonalini Khetrapal and other colleagues from ADB's Health Sector Group.

The report benefited from an external review team comprised of Rachel Silverman Bonnifield (Center for Global Development), Shoshanna Goldin (World Health Organization), Hyuncheol Bryant Kim (Hong Kong University of Science and Technology), and Gina Samaan (World Health Organization). The report also benefited from feedback by ADB staff who joined the workshops where the 13 background papers and draft report were presented, and participants of the 4th Asian Workshop on Econometrics and Health Economics in 2023, especially Professor Yoko Ibuka (Keio University, Japan), Matteo Lanzafame and Akihito Watabe (ADB).

Guy Sacerdoti edited the report and Alvin Tubio did the typesetting and graphics. Editha Laviña, Dyann Buenazedacruz, Heili Ann Bravo, and Pennylane Dela Cruz provided administrative support, proofreading, and further checks. The cover was designed by Erickson Mercado. A team from the Department of Communications and Knowledge Management, led by Terje Langeland, supported the report's dissemination.

DEFINITIONS

In this report, **Developing Asia** includes the 46 members of the Asian Development Bank listed below by geographic group

- **Association of Southeast Asian Nations** (ASEAN) includes Brunei Darussalam, Cambodia, Indonesia, the Lao People's Democratic Republic, Malaysia, Myanmar, the Philippines, Singapore, Thailand, and Viet Nam.

- **Caucasus and Central Asia** includes Armenia, Azerbaijan, Georgia, Kazakhstan, the Kyrgyz Republic, Tajikistan, Turkmenistan, and Uzbekistan.

- **East Asia** includes Hong Kong, China; Mongolia; the People's Republic of China; the Republic of Korea; and Taipei,China.

- **South Asia** includes Afghanistan, Bangladesh, Bhutan, India, Maldives, Nepal, Pakistan, and Sri Lanka.

- **Southeast Asia** includes Brunei Darussalam, Cambodia, Indonesia, the Lao People's Democratic Republic, Malaysia, Myanmar, the Philippines, Singapore, Thailand, Timor-Leste, and Viet Nam.

- **The Pacific** includes the Cook Islands, the Federated States of Micronesia, Fiji, Kiribati, the Marshall Islands, Nauru, Niue, Palau, Papua New Guinea, Samoa, Solomon Islands, Tonga, Tuvalu, and Vanuatu.

Unless otherwise specified, the symbol "$" refers to United States dollars.

ABBREVIATIONS

ADB	Asian Development Bank
ASEAN	Association of Southeast Asian Nations
CAREC	Central Asia Regional Economic Cooperation
COVID-19	coronavirus disease
ECDC	European Centre for Disease Prevention and Control
FSM	Federated States of Micronesia
GDP	gross domestic product
GHSI	Global Health Security Index
GSI	Google Search Index
ICU	intensive care unit
iGOT	Integrated Government Online Training platform
IMF	International Monetary Fund
Lao PDR	Lao People's Democratic Republic
MCM	medical countermeasures
MERS	Middle East respiratory syndrome
mRNA	messenger ribonucleic acid
NPI	non-pharmaceutical interventions
OECD	Organisation for Economic Co-operation and Development
PRC	People's Republic of China
PWB	psychological well-being
TE	technical efficiency
WHO	World Health Organization

What has COVID-19 Taught Us About Asia's Health Emergency Preparedness and Response?

The COVID-19 Pandemic Inflicted an Enormous Cost

The COVID-19 pandemic caused unprecedented economic disruption. The pandemic resulted in the largest global economic crisis since the Great Depression in the 1930s (section 2). The crisis increased poverty and widened inequality within and across economies. Evidence suggests that many economies, particularly developing economies, will take a long time to recover fully from these losses.

Prior to the development and roll-out of COVID-19 vaccines, governments relied on non-pharmaceutical interventions (NPIs), which stymied many economies. Given the worries and uncertainties during the first few months of the pandemic, many economies imposed large-scale lockdowns and school closures. Only essential workers and services were allowed to continue. Empirical evidence shows that these stringent NPIs led to significant economic disruptions. They resulted in large reductions in GDP per capita and increased unemployment rates, even in the medium term after restrictions were loosened. Recovering fully from these disruptions will take many years, especially in developing economies. Learning losses, the dropping out of many workers from the labor force, and the necessity for governments to increase public debt to support the economy have compounded the challenges. While NPIs saved lives, some appeared more cost effective than others (section 5).

NPIs and the pandemic also reduced people's psychological well-being. Significant heterogeneity in the effect on psychological well-being across economies in Asia and the Pacific was caused directly by the pandemic itself and NPI stringency, and indirectly through resultant higher unemployment and declining livelihoods. Among economies whose citizens suffered the highest drop in psychological well-being, NPI stringency was positively associated with depressive symptoms.

Lengthy school closures resulted in large learning losses, damaging future economic prospects. Evidence shows that longer school closures generally resulted in larger learning losses and consistently increased learning inequality. While most schools had reopened by February 2022, the evidence shows most education systems returned to business as usual, rather than striving to rapidly recover lost learning. Thus, there is a high risk of permanent scarring, which significantly lowers the lifetime income of the students who experienced school closures. In addition, school closures aggravated pre-existing learning poverty, as well as learning gaps between rich and poor children.

The COVID-19 Pandemic Found Health Systems both Fragile and Unprepared

Health systems in most economies had not previously focused on or prepared for a pandemic. The emergence and uncontrolled spread of COVID-19 revealed the gaps in national and international approaches to pandemic preparedness. It sent a strong signal that traditional measures of preparedness were not necessarily associated with pandemic response or outcome. The historic underinvestment in modernizing core public health functions was clear—such as in surveillance, reporting, communications, and coordination. There were not enough public health laboratories available, or infrastructure for delivering essential care.

Health security capacities are crucial to prevent, detect, and respond to emergencies. The adequacy of health systems should be monitored regularly. According to an ADB study done in 2021, economies able to successfully contain the pandemic were those that involved diverse expertise, multiple sectors, and a broad set of actors in decision-making and forging responses. These economies reacted swiftly and aggressively, following the lessons learned from previous emergency and crisis planning, management, coordination, and response. Across the region, the success of the Republic of Korea with testing and digital contact tracing stood out; along with Thailand in prevention, detection, and reporting cases; and Viet Nam's focus on prevention, as it registered fewer than 2,000 COVID-19 cases from the start of the pandemic through December 2020. Some economies like the Republic of Korea; New Zealand; Japan; Australia; and Hong Kong, China limited virus transmission at the start of the pandemic by carefully calibrating and effectively implementing NPI measures.

Some governments addressed their health system limitations as the pandemic progressed. Although the pandemic in general overwhelmed health systems, the Republic of Korea, the People's Republic of China, and Indonesia were able to significantly boost capacity, for example, using technology such as telemedicine and mobile-based contact tracing. They were able to effectively triage, sending non-critical cases to home care while reserving hospital space for critical patients. India, for example, was able to repurpose industrial oxygen for medical use. Important determining factors for an effective response include sustained investment in health systems, adequate funding for primary healthcare, and universal health coverage.

There was unequal access to medical countermeasures, including vaccines. Many economies did not have the manufacturing capacity or approval process for producing medical countermeasures during emergencies, such as surgical masks and oxygen. Vaccine doses obtained by some economies were 8 to 10 times their population, while others, usually developing economies, could not secure enough to vaccinate their population once. While developed economies were able to secure vaccine supplies within 100 days of the March 2020 designation of the pandemic, many developing economies needed more than 300 days. Developing economies also faced significant challenges in quickly vaccinating their people.

Data Limitations Constrained Governments' Ability to Implement Effective Policies

Rapidly updated data, data wrangling, and data analysis are key to handling health emergencies. Data capabilities allow policymakers to conduct near real-time assessments, make informed decisions, and rapidly evaluate and correct course if needed. Suggestive evidence produced for this report shows that better data infrastructure helped reduce the severity of the pandemic. Access to broadband internet also lessened the impact of COVID-19.

Health-related data in many developing member economies are limited and outdated. Of ADB's 46 developing members, about half provide official data on the number of health facilities or equipment available. And even for these, most data were last updated more than a decade ago. During the pandemic, much critical data were largely missing or sparse, for example, data on available hospital beds or intensive care unit occupancy. Disaggregated data by sex, income group, age, or morbidity were virtually non-existent. Routinely collected administrative data are filed away, used mainly by the government agency that collected them. Data are not readily linkable across agencies.

The rapidly evolving COVID-19 variants combined with data deficiencies may have led to ineffective or inefficient policies. Infrequently updated government data systems were incompatible with the speed at which variants spread. Data were not standardized, and quality depended on local capabilities. This implied variations in reliability and validity of data, resulting in a high risk of misinterpretation.

Lessons from the COVID-19 Pandemic

Economies with efficient health systems were better able to handle the pandemic. Evidence shows that economies with higher health system efficiency—measured by their ability to translate inputs such as health expenditure per person into desired outputs such as longer life expectancy and lower infant mortality—had higher vaccination coverage and lower mortality during the pandemic. They were able to test more of their population and implemented more rigorous contact tracing. Their quarantine process was also more effective and, in some cases, humane. This implies that adequate investment in healthcare infrastructure and utilization are the foundation of health emergency preparedness.

Pharmaceutical interventions were more cost effective than NPIs. Consistently, vaccinations were highly cost effective across many different economies. School closures had the lowest cost-effectiveness because of their limited success in reducing contact and the high long-term cost from learning loss. Evidence also shows that mixing policy interventions increased the cost-effectiveness of NPIs, rather than relying on a single NPI. Economies should experiment until they find the most cost-effective mix for their specific context—they should not copy the policy mix of economies facing different circumstances. In setting NPI goals, policymakers must consider both the direct benefit (reducing infections) and indirect costs (economic, social, and psychological). Real-time feedback on their effectiveness is critically important, with many economies finding it an enormous challenge.

Coordination and partnerships played a vital role in delivering COVID-19 responses. Unprecedented crises like the COVID-19 pandemic call for coordinated responses domestically, regionally, and globally. Successful implementation of pandemic response programs was attributed to broad partnerships, close coordination, flexibility, and risk-taking. Within an economy, coordination and clear communications among those dealing with the pandemic, including government agencies and private entities, are key to ensure effective interventions. Governments must also work closely with international organizations and development partners. Continuous dialogue and participatory approaches among institutions involved facilitates effective program design and co-financing that help address implementation challenges.

Key Policy Takeaways

Determining the efficient level of health emergency preparedness is empirically very difficult. Preparedness for COVID-19 is distinct from preparedness, for example, for an Ebola outbreak, given the different nature of the pathogens. The kinds of preparedness needed to respond to chemical leaks or bioterrorism attacks also differ. Investing to prepare for all health emergencies is both unaffordable and an inefficient use of scarce public resources. Authorities should strategically choose how they should prepare for emergencies. The choice may depend on the emergency's frequency, likelihood, and predictability. More importantly, strengthening certain aspects of the public health system would improve preparedness for all health emergencies.

The lessons from the COVID-19 pandemic underscore the importance of prioritizing investments in healthcare infrastructure and preparedness. Enhancing the overall efficiency of health systems is crucial, as economies with more efficient systems managed the pandemic better. Policymakers should focus on improving technical efficiency, increasing access to healthcare services, and addressing disparities through strategic planning and resource allocation. In addition, a strong emphasis on data-driven decision-making and early response strategies highlights the value of data in containing a health emergency. Tailoring interventions for a specific economy, prioritizing pharmaceutical interventions in health emergencies, and integrating crisis response into macroeconomic policies are needed for an effective and context-specific response. The importance of flexibility, innovation, collaboration, and continuous investment in building scientific knowledge for future health emergencies can hardly be overemphasized to enhance resilience and response capabilities.

Increase health system preparedness as it cannot be improved overnight or during an emergency.
Efforts to build a robust system should begin during normal times. This means building an established supply chain and health workforce with knowledge of disease transmission and vaccine delivery. While many governments invested and built up capacities in testing laboratories, contact tracing, and quarantine facilities during the pandemic, many found their healthcare infrastructure and emergency medical supplies could not keep up with the surge in demand. Technological and innovation capacities varied with respect to the production and distribution of pharmaceutical and non-pharmaceutical health products. They also varied widely across and within rich, middle-income, and lower-income economies. And they were concentrated in advanced countries in Europe and North America. Some Asian economies, due to their quick response and robust public health system, handled the pandemic effectively early on in terms of disease transmission, clinical care, and reduced mortality. Others, especially those with weaker systems, faced greater challenges. Healthcare delivery systems, particularly in primary healthcare, need to be strengthened as part of pandemic preparedness. Any limitations could prevent people from quickly accessing many types of preventive care.

Strengthen data infrastructure, harness available administrative data, and establish supporting regulations for data sharing. These data issues are the foundation that allows researchers and government agencies to access more data, conduct more accurate analysis, and support better policies and decisions. Governments could also rely on non-traditional data sources, including big data from the private sector and citizen-generated data. Finally, using advanced techniques like machine learning, supported by big data, could improve the predictive accuracy of contagion during health emergencies. It also allows policymakers to rapidly evaluate their policies.

Balance trade-offs when implementing NPIs. NPIs should maximize the benefits of preventing infections while considering intervention costs. While stringent NPIs have been associated with lower COVID-19 mortality rates, they also led to large economic contractions, reductions in psychological well-being, and substantial learning losses. Acknowledging and calculating the trade-offs between protecting public health and minimizing disruptions would help policymakers better balance the NPI impact.

Rely on flexibility, innovation, and collaboration in future health emergencies. These aspects require an adequately funded health system, well-equipped infrastructure, along with motivated and skilled personnel. They also require nimble data gathering, sharing, and analysis that help inform policies. There is also a need to establish strategic partnerships with different stakeholders that hold unique comparative advantage.

Four years have passed since the World Health Organization (WHO) declared COVID-19 a global pandemic. The pandemic exposed health system deficiencies, resulting in millions of deaths and long-term illnesses. It is important to document and learn from this experience. WHO (2023) highlights the importance of interconnectedness in health emergency responses, noting that no one is safe until everyone is safe. Pandemic preparedness and responses need to consider that "health is everyone's business", and that responses need to be "agile and adaptive." This leads to the One Health approach, in which a broader set of stakeholders is needed to respond effectively to biological and environmental threats (McKimm et al. 2023). Also, as the WHO report and European Centre for Disease Prevention and Control (ECDC 2023) both emphasize, economies should invest in functional capacities, interoperable systems, and critical health infrastructure. Effective coordination between central authorities, local authorities, and communities is also crucial to map out medical supplies and health workers. Narayanasamy et al. (2023) adds that pandemic preparedness requires collaboration between academia, government, and industry; better pathogen diagnostics; and a high level of trust in science. Multilateral systems also need to strengthen as national governments widen universal health coverage in their respective economies (Sachs et al. 2022).

This report highlights the lessons learned from the pandemic. Drawing on the experience of economies in Asia and the Pacific, it adds to the existing body of knowledge by systematically examining elements of health emergency preparedness, highlighting data limitations that constrained governments in rapidly evaluating and adapting their policies during the pandemic, and measuring the cost-effectiveness of both pharmaceutical and non-pharmaceutical interventions. These lessons are important to bolster preparedness and better respond to future health emergencies.

The report is based on in-depth empirical analyses of aspects of the pandemic and government responses. The 13 background papers that informed this report cover a wide range of topics (see page 41). They estimate the impact of non-pharmaceutical interventions (NPIs) on economic growth; track psychological well-being (PWB) during lockdowns and the effects of stringent policies; estimate the impact of having better access to technology; calculate health system efficiency prior to the pandemic and how it correlates with numbers of cases or deaths; compare the cost-effectiveness of different NPIs and pharmaceutical interventions; simulate the impact of applying different intervention mixes; and discuss the controversies surrounding excess mortality. One background paper focuses on the lack of data availability and sharing as a major constraint to an effective pandemic response. Another demonstrates the use of machine learning in providing policymakers quicker and better information on effective interventions. And one reviews responses of the Asian Development Bank (ADB) and individual economies.

The report is necessarily limited in scope. The report aims to identify key lessons to prepare for future health emergencies, focusing particularly on areas where ADB support can be useful. It does not attempt to offer a comprehensive analysis of all elements of the COVID-19 response, many of which were highly political, context-specific, and remain contested even after several years. For example, the report refrains from delving into a deep technical discussion of what has been covered by the WHO (2023), like the disease pathogen aspect of COVID-19, One Health, and the differences between vaccines (e.g., mRNA vs other methods). The impact on global trade, tourism, international travel and logistics, as well as the disproportional impact on gender are largely excluded. While the analyses and lessons focus on Asia and the Pacific, the recommendations and lessons can be useful for policymakers in other regions.

2 COVID-19 Inflicted Enormous Costs

The pandemic caused significant loss of life, welfare, psychological well-being, and education. The COVID-19 pandemic affected lives and livelihoods globally, and caused almost 7 million deaths by mid-2023 (Figure 2.1). However, when considering a measure of excess mortality, the actual number of deaths associated with COVID-19 was about three times higher than officially reported.[1] The pandemic caused unprecedented economic disruption across the world, leading to a major global economic crisis (Abiad et al. 2020; World Bank 2022; ADB 2022). Gross domestic product (GDP) growth rates declined across Asia as COVID-19 started to spread in 2020 (Figure 2.2). The economic crisis increased poverty and inequality within and across economies, with evidence suggesting that many, particularly emerging and poorer economies, will require considerable time to recover from pandemic-induced economic losses (World Bank 2022). Aside from the devastating impact on lives and the economy, the COVID-19 pandemic imposed a huge toll on people's psychological well-being. School closures resulted in substantial losses in education and aggravated pre-existing learning poverty across many parts of the world. There is also evidence suggesting that the negative impact on social capital by lowering trust due to social distancing also increased social isolation (Alizadeh et al. 2023).

2.1 COVID-19 Policy Responses Imposed Substantial Economic Costs

NPIs during the early stage of the pandemic were costly. Before vaccines arrived and effective protection and treatment known, governments had to rely heavily on NPIs, albeit to varying degrees. Travel restrictions, school and business closures, and stay-at-home orders were used to control the spread of the virus. Economies with more stringent NPIs during this early phase had lower COVID-19 mortality rates (Flaxman et al. 2020; Hale et al. 2021). Although these restrictions were aimed at minimizing deaths, illness and other adverse health effects, there were substantial economic and social costs (Hale et al. 2021).

Economies all over the world contracted due to NPIs, particularly lockdowns. Early evidence on the economic impact of COVID-19 lockdowns—during the first few months of government-imposed mobility restrictions—suggests damaging economic effects (König and Winkler 2021; Deb et al. 2022). In the Republic of Korea, for example, Shin et al. (2021) show that the effects of less intense but more targeted temporary business closures differ by underlying geographical characteristics. Based on the economic impact of past pandemics, Emmerling et al. (2021) predict declining GDP per capita along with an increase in poverty and inequality will last until at least 2025.

---

[1] There is controversy over the data on COVID-19 mortality, as the number of related deaths is estimated to be more than double official reports (Malik 2024). In many economies, cumulative excess deaths—the difference between predicted and officially reported deaths—is massive with undercounting more prominent in low-income economies (COVID-19 Excess Mortality Collaborators 2022).

Figure 2.1 COVID-19 Cases and Deaths: January 2020 to July 2023

The COVID-19 pandemic had a dramatic impact on lives and livelihoods.

Legend:
- Asia
- Africa
- Europe
- North America
- Oceania
- South America
- Total deaths ——

Daily cases, million | Total deaths, million

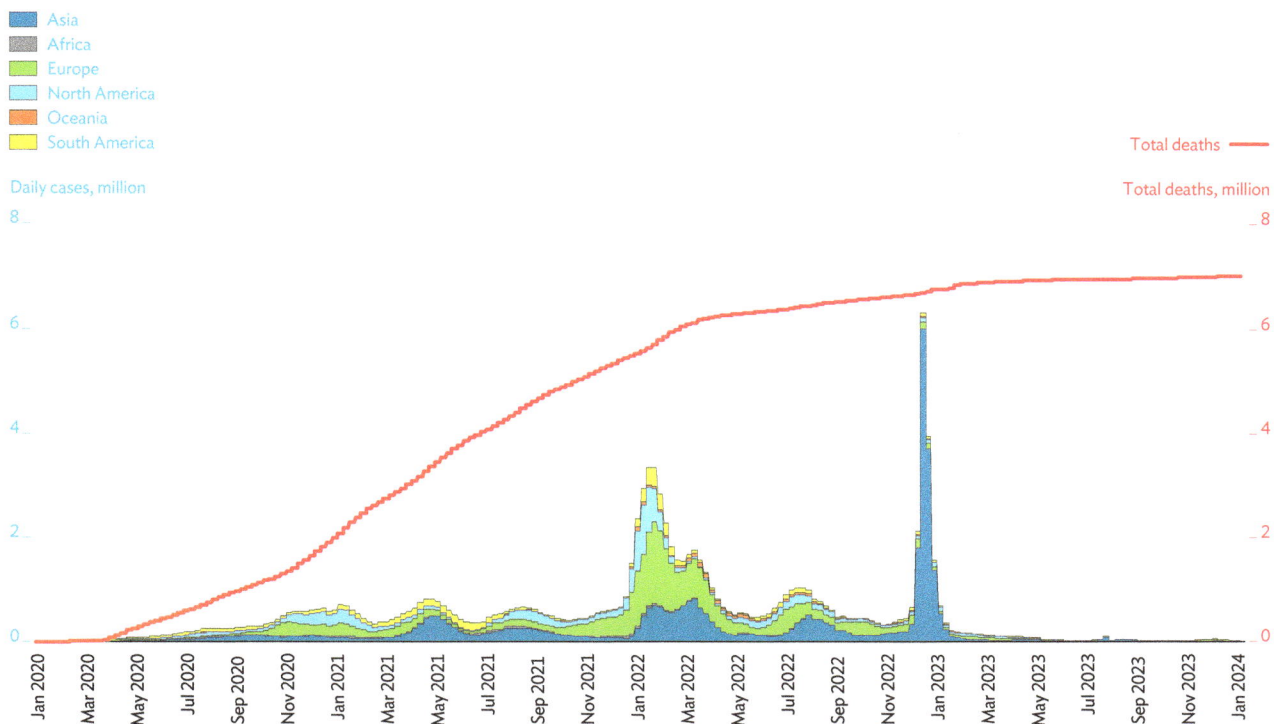

Source: Our World in Data.

Figure 2.2 Annual GDP Growth Rate

Growth rates across Asia fell sharply as COVID-19 spread in 2020, and developing Asia experienced its first outright contraction in 6 decades.

Legend:
- 2019
- 2020
- 2021

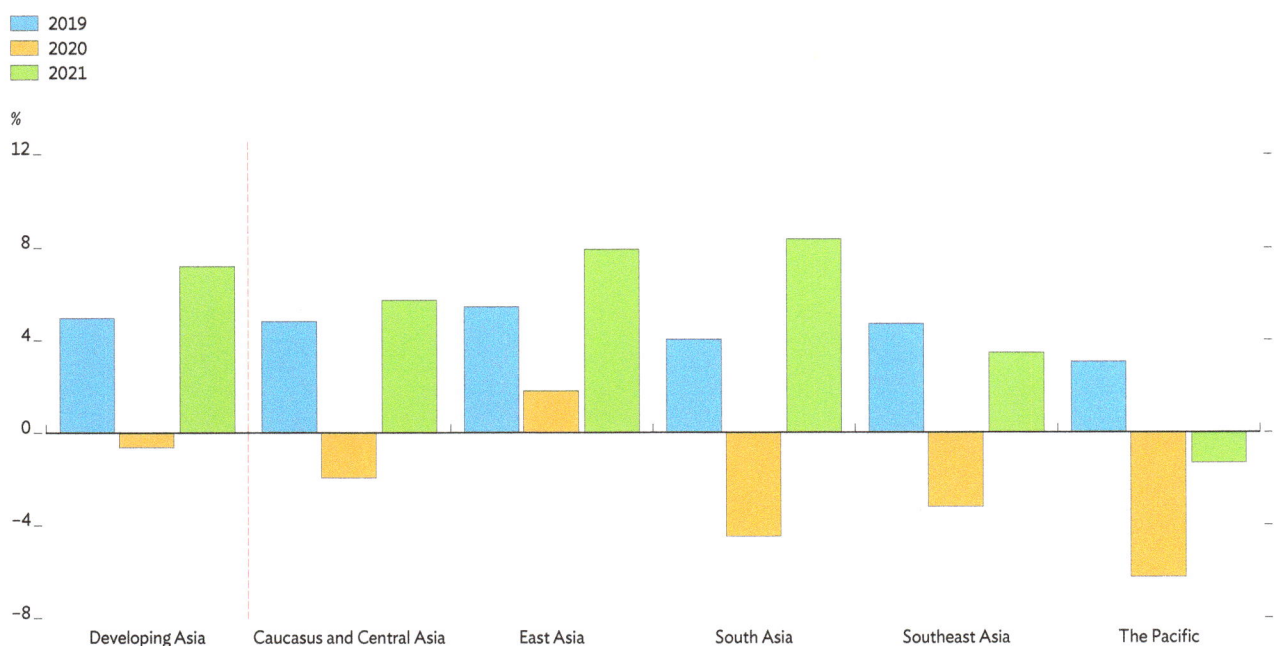

GDP = gross domestic product.
Source: *Asian Development Outlook* database.

The study suggests that travel restrictions, lockdowns, and social distancing during the pandemic affected global value chains more than in the past and will have a lasting economic impact. It also projects an increase in the public debt to GDP ratio—with implications on debt sustainability for many economies. By contrast, Ashraf and Goodell (2022) investigates the impact lockdowns and social distancing had on quarterly GDP among Organisation for Economic Co-operation and Development members, and found that despite short-run damage to economic activity, the restrictions increased the chances for stronger economic recovery over the medium-term.

Governments with stricter NPIs tended to see larger reductions in GDP per capita. Using NPI data from 2020–2021, Kim et al. (2024b) show that government NPIs such as mobility restrictions were accompanied by deteriorating economic growth. They examined the relationships between government-imposed NPIs and macroeconomic outcomes—such as GDP per capita and the unemployment rate—using panel data from 165 economies. Using data for 2011–2021, GDP declined immediately at the start of the pandemic (Figure 2.3). The upward trend returned during the second year of the pandemic but remained lower than its pre-pandemic trajectory, suggesting that government NPIs might have prevented economies from returning to their pre-pandemic trend.

This implies the possibility that the negative impacts of NPIs would last longer than expected. This is also observed in terms of unemployment rate and output loss. The analysis suggests that the adverse NPI impact on an economy was mainly driven by school closures, workplace closures, and international travel bans. NPIs affected foot traffic by reducing the daily number of visitors to various locations, which reduces consumption spending and labor supply. The interventions initially came as temporary supply and demand shocks, lowering economic activity and growth.

Heterogeneous impacts were observed across economies depending on NPI intensity. A quicker recovery occurred in economies with very mild or very intense restrictions during the first year of the pandemic. Asian economies generally experienced relatively mild economic losses compared with the rest of the world, but they did not seem to recover from these losses any quicker. This suggests heterogeneity in the impact government restrictions had on economies, which implies that the economic impact of NPIs was largely determined by the economy's underlying economic condition. The contemporaneous relationship between NPI stringency and GDP per capita was largely linear, implying that economies that applied more stringent NPI measures lost more GDP per capita (Figure 2.4, Panel A).

Figure 2.3 Global and Regional GDP Relative to Pre-pandemic Trends, 2016–2023

GDP dropped well below trend in 2020 and had not recovered even by 2023.

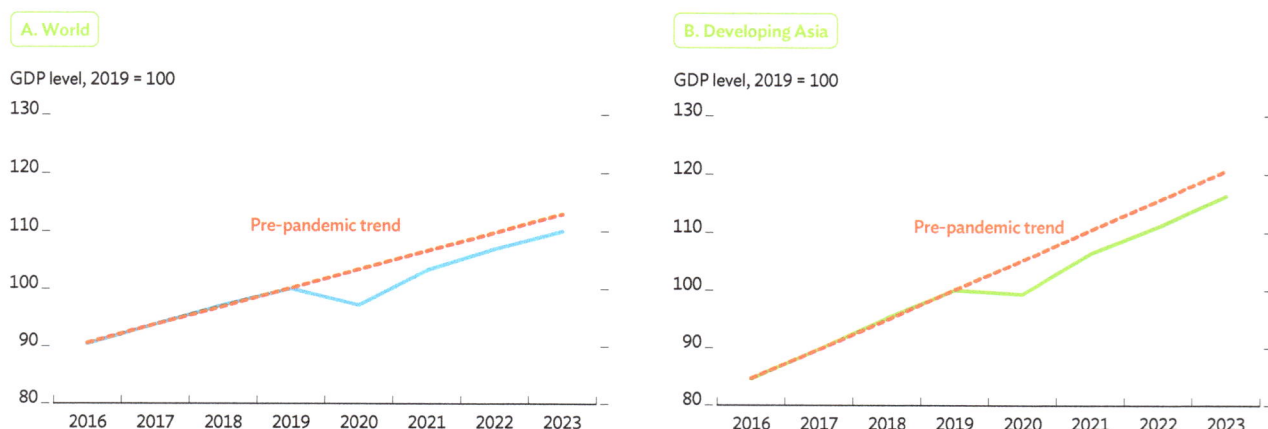

GDP = gross domestic product.
Note: Pre-pandemic trend line is computed using 2016–2019 data.
Source: Asian Development Bank estimates using data from *Asian Development Outlook September 2023* and IMF *World Economic Outlook October 2023* database.

Figure 2.4 Mobility Restrictions and GDP per Capita

NPI stringency suppressed output but did not necessarily promote faster recovery.

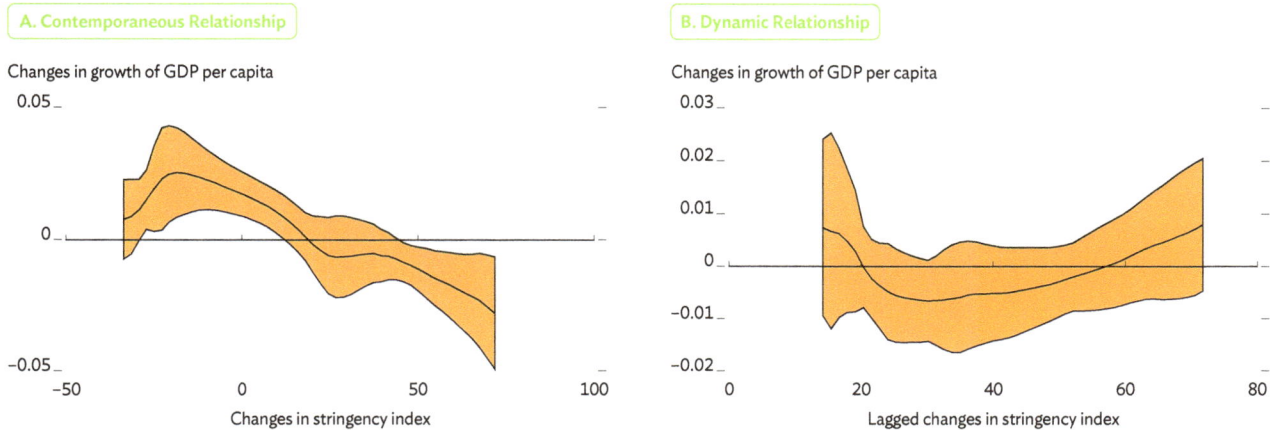

GDP = gross domestic product; NPI = non-pharmaceutical interventions.

Notes: Panel A—a regression of GDP growth per capita is estimated on lagged growth of GDP per capita, log value of GDP per capita as of 2019, the difference in the annual average of the number of daily deaths per million, and the difference in vaccination rates; the smoothed relationships between changes in growth of GDP per capita and the change in stringency index are plotted using the running-mean smoother and a bandwidth of 10.
Panel B—For the dynamic relationship, the same panel A regression is estimated adding the lagged changes in stringency index as an independent variable, after which the change in growth of GDP per capita is calculated. The shaded areas indicate 95% confidence intervals.

Sources: Kim et al. 2024b; Our World in Data; World Bank. World Development Indicators; Oxford COVID-19 Government Response Tracker.

There is also an indication of a U-shaped dynamic relationship between the NPI stringency and economic recovery. Generally, however, stricter NPIs did not appear to accelerate economic recovery a year after they were imposed (Figure 2.4, Panel B). Overall, the non-linear pattern does not appear to come with a high degree of certainty, suggesting that economic gains from mobility restrictions only mildly outweighed their economic costs—including the larger health costs associated with less strict NPIs. Meanwhile, vaccination rates during this period were positively associated with growth outcomes.

2.2 Pandemic Worsens Economic Well-being

COVID-19 exposed weaknesses in economic resilience across the globe. According to the World Development Report 2022 (World Bank 2022), more than half of the households in emerging and advanced economies were unable to sustain basic consumption for more than 3 months if they lost income due to the pandemic. The average business could cover less than 55 days of expenses (or about 2 months)

using cash reserves. Given the disruptions in incomes and business, many households and firms struggled to service their pre-pandemic debt, thus reducing their well-being. ADB (2022) suggests that the fight against poverty in developing Asia stopped for 2 years with many finding it harder than before to escape poverty. World Bank (2022) suggests that global poverty increased for the first time in a generation, and that existing inequality was fueled further by disproportionate income losses among marginal populations. Youth, women, the self-employed, and casual workers with lower levels of formal education suffered from income losses more, and women were affected most due to lockdowns. Temporary unemployment rose in 70% of economies for workers with only a primary education in 2020. The report also suggests that businesses—including smaller firms, informal businesses, and those with limited access to formal credit—were hit harder by income losses, and that micro-, small, and medium sized enterprises were most severely affected in sectors like accommodation and food services, retail, and personal services.

Many economies with pre-existing economic weaknesses suffered more from the COVID-19 impact. Kodama et al. (2023), using representative household surveys from 17 members of the Association of Southeast Asian Nations (ASEAN) and the Central Asia Regional Economic Cooperation (CAREC) Program, conclude that household family businesses were hurt by COVID-19 and related policy restrictions. During 2020, 58.7% of ASEAN family business households and 41.4% of CAREC's lost income, while 4.1% of those in ASEAN and 7.1% in CAREC were forced to close. The study finds that government financial assistance helped mitigate these adverse effects. Tanaka (2022) documents that the shocks among households and workers in Asia were heterogeneous and that job losses due to lockdowns were more evident among lower-educated and lower-income groups, with losses in income felt by low-skilled workers as well as women.

Governments, along with international and multilateral organizations, responded with major economic policy support packages to mitigate the short-term, pandemic-induced economic costs. Governments used various fiscal measures, including household cash transfers, business stimulus payments, along with wage and rent subsidies to mitigate some of the impact (Tabuga 2024; Gentilini 2022; Chetty et al. 2020; Kubota et al. 2021). Studies show these policies were effective in mitigating the negative economic impacts of the pandemic. According to Gentilini (2022), these cash transfers helped reduce poverty and prevent households from falling into extreme poverty.

There are concerns over the future effectiveness and sustainability of pandemic-related fiscal measures. Direct transfers and spending coupons may not be sustainable over the long term and may result in inflationary pressures if not carefully managed. Wage and rent subsidies may be difficult to implement equitably and may result in firms receiving support they do not need. In addition, while stimulus payments may be effective in the short term, they may not address the underlying structural issues contributing to economic slowdowns (Kim et al. 2024b). According to World Bank (2022), the emergency response resulted in increased private and public debt globally. Decisive action will be needed to address the debt challenge. It also suggests that policymakers must identify those measures that are sustainable, effective, and equitable over the long term.

2.3 COVID-19 Imposed a Heavy Toll on Psychological Well-being

Apart from the devastating impact on lives and the economy, the pandemic imposed a huge toll on PWB. COVID deaths and the grief for those losing loved ones added to psychological distress and mental illness (Joaquim et al. 2021). Government NPIs— such as national lockdowns, closures of non-essential workplaces and schools, limited daily mobility and social gatherings—significantly and persistently disrupted daily activities. However, NPI stringency does not necessarily coincide with individual behavior—many people acted as if they were under severe restrictions even if they were not legally required to do so. In addition, the spikes in COVID-19 cases due to the delta and omicron variants forced many economies previously considered highly successful in containing the virus to reintroduce strict social distancing, reducing hope of returning to a normal pre-pandemic life.

COVID-19 had a negative impact on mental health, according to early attempts to investigate its effect on PWB. Aksunger et al. (2023), using a prospective cohort study, compare mental health in eight low- and middle-income economies in Asia, Africa and South America. They find that depressive symptoms significantly increased in the first 4 months of the pandemic, suggesting that COVID-19 might induce long-term depression in economies with poor mental health support facilities. Other studies also find negative effects on PWB, focusing mainly on the short-term impact during the pandemic's early phase within a particular Western country setting—such as a well-defined population segment in a single country (Wang and Zhao 2020; Vindegaard and Benros 2020; Xiong et al. 2020; Brodeur et al. 2021).

The PWB trend during 2019–2022 was heterogenous in Asia. By leveraging Google's high-frequency search data on depressive symptoms, Kim et al. (2024a) provide insights into the changes in PWB from the search intensity of depressive symptoms.[2] Of 34 Asian economies in the sample, eight—Bangladesh, Bhutan, India, Indonesia, Mongolia, Nepal, Pakistan, and Sri Lanka—

---

2   The composite search intensity index for each economy used the following search terms: feeling, sad, depressed, depression, impairment, insomnia, empty, feeling worthless, feeling guilty, and suicide.

had significant PWB losses during the early pandemic stage, while others saw a relatively mild decline. For these eight countries, the data show that peaks of government NPI stringency and COVID-19 severity occurred at the different stages of the pandemic (Figure 2.5). The severity of government restrictions occurred early in the pandemic and gradually decreased over time. However, the health risk of COVID-19 (measured by deaths per million people) was highest in mid-2021, when the delta variant quickly became dominant in many economies. Also, the trend of stringency index confirms that governments periodically adjusted the intensity of NPIs depending on the changing COVID-19 situation—the trend in deaths per million does not show such strong seasonality of COVID-19 severity. The trends of the Google Search Index (GSI) on depressive symptoms and the number of COVID-19 deaths per million in these countries show that the GSI for depressive symptoms surged during the first wave in mid-2020 and then again in mid-2021 during the delta variant second wave (Figure 2.6). The search intensity was stronger during the first wave, although the number of COVID-19 deaths was much smaller than the second wave.

NPIs negatively affected PWB. Overall, government stringency enforcement, controlling for pandemic severity, significantly affected PWB across Asia (Kim et al. 2024a). Restricting the analysis to eight Asian countries that experienced sharp reductions in PWB during the early stages of the pandemic, the study examined relationships between the stringency of government NPIs and PWB based on the regression analysis of GSI and stringency index on the number of COVID-19 deaths per million and year-month fixed effects, respectively. There was a roughly linear relationship between the residuals of GSI and the NPI stringency index, suggesting that depressive symptoms worsen with stricter NPIs (Figure 2.7). There were three main findings: (i) significant heterogeneity in changes in PWB occurred during COVID-19 across economies, implying that not every economy saw a large surge in depressive symptoms during the initial phase; (ii) stringency in government NPIs were positively associated with depressive symptoms—a one unit increase in the government stringency index is associated with a 0.01 standard deviation increase in the GSI of depressive symptoms, and; (iii) people's anticipation of stricter government restrictions could worsen their mental health.

Figure 2.5 Trends of Stringency Index and Number of Deaths per Million during COVID-19

The stringency index peaked much earlier than the number of deaths due to the virus.

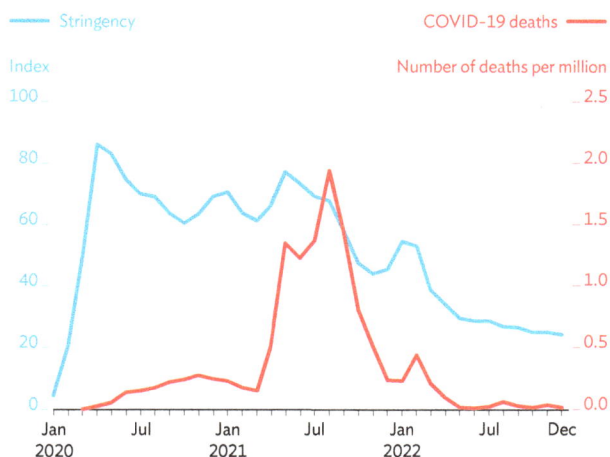

Sources: Kim et al. 2024a; Our World in Data; Oxford COVID-19 Government Response Tracker.

Figure 2.6 Trends of Google Search Index Data on Depressive Symptoms and Number of Deaths per Million during COVID-19

Depressive symptoms surged significantly during the first and the second waves of COVID-19.

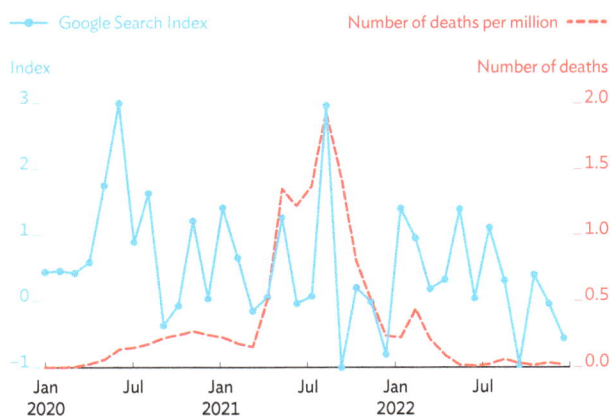

Sources: Kim et al. 2024a; Google's Search Index Data on Depressive Symptoms (eight Asian countries); Oxford COVID-19 Government Response Tracker.

The trend of GSI begins to rise at least 2 months before an increase in NPI stringency and reductions in PWB are significant and persistent over the next 3 months. This suggests that PWB started to worsen when stricter NPIs were anticipated, and the impact could persist at least for 3 months after the NPIs were implemented.

Figure 2.7 Google Search Index on Depressive Symptoms and COVID-19 Stringency Index

Depressive symptoms worsen with stricter NPIs.

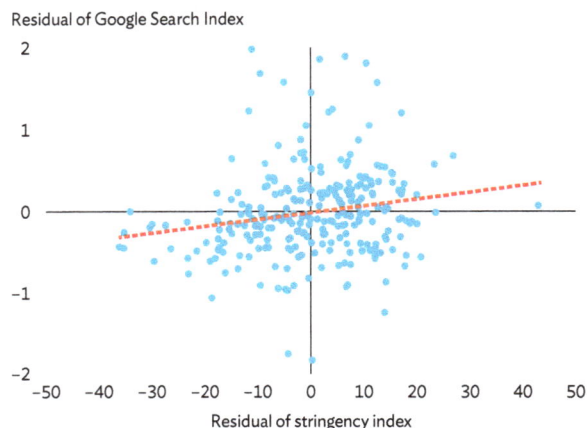

Residual of Google Search Index

NPI = non-pharmaceutical intervention.

Sources: Kim et al. 2024a; Google Trend Data (eight countries); Oxford COVID-19 Government Response Tracker.

2.4 School Closures Had a Devastating Impact on Learning

COVID-19 resulted in the longest school closures in recent history. The COVID-19 pandemic caused governments to shut down schools amid other restrictive measures to contain infection risk, resulting in the longest school closures in recent history. Global evidence suggests that on average, students lost half a year's worth of learning (Jakubowski et al. 2023). Schools in developing Asia on average were closed for as long as 272 instruction days (73% of school days) between February 2020 and October 2021, with the average length between 42 days in the Pacific to 375 days in South Asia (Molato-Gayares and Thomas 2022).

School closures led to significant learning loss, which hurts future economic prospects. Molato-Gayares and Thomas (2022) provide an account of learning loss across developing Asia, suggesting that children's learning in almost all sample economies fell substantially during the pandemic compared with the pre-pandemic period. Maddawin et al. (2024) report that 80% of parents in Southeast Asia felt that their children learned significantly less than before the pandemic.

The meta-analysis done by Dela Cruz et al. (2024), which contains the highest number of studies from developing economies than others, finds that every year of school closure reduced learning by 1.1 years (Figure 2.8). Reopening schools helped learning recovery, but a learning loss of 0.5 years persists, implying that long-term scarring is highly likely.

Figure 2.8 COVID-19 School Closures and Learning Loss

The longer the school closes, the larger the learning loss.

Learning loss (equivalent school year), residualized

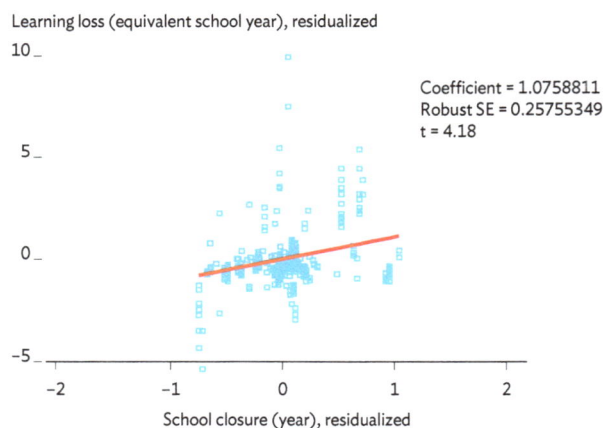

Coefficient = 1.0758811
Robust SE = 0.25755349
t = 4.18

School closure (year), residualized

Notes: The plot is a graphical representation of the weighted regression results in Table 3 (column 4) of Dela Cruz et al. (2024). The residual of schooling years closed is graphed with the residual of learning loss after removing the effect of school reopening, education level, subject, development status, access to remote learning, and pre-pandemic learning outcomes. The slope corresponds to the relationship between length of school closure and years of learning lost in the absence of reopening.

Source: Asian Development Bank estimates using data from Dela Cruz et al. 2024.

COVID-19 school closures not only resulted in substantial learning loss, but also aggravated pre-existing learning poverty and widened learning gaps. According to a new report by the World Bank, UNESCO, UNICEF, the United Kingdom's Foreign, Commonwealth & Development Office, USAID, and the Bill & Melinda Gates Foundation (2022), learning poverty increased by almost one-third in low- and middle-income economies—70% of 10-year-olds were "unable to understand a simple written text," compared with a pre-COVID estimate of 57% in 2019 (World Bank 2022). The report states that the same generation of students "risks losing $21 trillion in potential lifetime earnings in present value, or the equivalent of 17% of today's global GDP, up from the $17 trillion estimated in 2021."

There is evidence that poor children suffered the most, with learning inequality rising due to unequal mitigation measures both during school closures and after re-opening. This will lead to widening income inequality in the future. Moscoviz and Evans (2022) review the effect on learning during the pandemic and suggest that students from poor families were affected more due to poor internet access or online learning, along with larger negative shocks to family income, which reduced their ability to support learning. This led to students returning to school with larger gaps in learning levels.

Scarring effects will likely cause significantly lower permanent income. The lost learning in schools affects a student's progression to higher levels, which will affect employability, productivity, earnings, and economic progress. Cohen et al. (2022) examine the medium- to long-term economic effects of school closures using a general equilibrium framework and find that the negative impact on GDP and employment worsens over time—from a 0.2% decline in 2024 to a 0.6% decline in 2028 and 1.1% in 2030. This suggests that the cost of school closures in absolute terms could be as much as $943 billion in 2030. In the absence of remedial measures for lost learning, it would result in substantial earnings loss—$3.2 trillion in lost lifetime earnings for students in developing Asia—equivalent to 13% of the region's GDP in 2020 (ADB 2022).

2.5 Policy Takeaways

Balance priorities on health and the economy when implementing NPIs. While stringent NPIs were associated with lower COVID-19 mortality rates, they also led to substantial economic contractions. In some economies, there is evidence that stringent NPIs were in place longer than necessary. As a result, some households suffered significant economic losses, non-COVID illnesses were not treated, depressive symptoms set in, and millions of children suffered learning losses. Adopting well-targeted and flexible NPIs would help policymakers minimize these costs while ensuring effective containment measures.

Ensure an equitable and inclusive economic recovery via targeted and sustainable economic support. The economic impact of COVID-19 disproportionately affected people and economies with pre-existing economic weaknesses. Policymakers should prioritize recovery strategies that address existing inequalities, considering the heterogeneity in the impact across different demographic and economic groups. Economic support measures, such as cash transfers and subsidies, should be targeted to effectively reach those most affected by a pandemic. However, there is also the need for a careful balance that ensures these interventions are sustainable. An inclusive recovery plan should not only focus on short-term relief but also address underlying structural issues contributing to economic slowdowns. This implies continually evaluating and adjusting policies to meet evolving economic challenges without compromising long-term fiscal stability.

Account for the mental health implications of pandemic control measures. Lockdowns and strict social distance measures, particularly during episodes of surging COVID-19 infections, damaged PWB across Asia. The stringency of government NPIs was shown to be positively associated with elevated depressive symptoms. This raises the need for a balanced approach that addresses the health risks of a pandemic while minimizing its adverse effects on PWB. This includes the flexibility to adjust NPI intensity based on the severity of the situation, which requires rapid evaluations to understand how PWB is affected and clear communications to manage people's anticipation of stricter government requirements. The potential long-term mental health challenge from stringent NPIs also highlights the need to establish and strengthen mental health support facilities and services.

Recover learning losses while raising learning equality. Prolonged school closures during the pandemic resulted in significant learning losses. The evidence underscores the urgency for governments and education authorities to implement effective and targeted educational recovery strategies crucial to mitigate the long-term implications on a student's educational attainment and future economic prospects. The educational damage from school closures also disproportionately affected poor children, widening learning inequality. Interventions that address these disparities will provide opportunities to mitigate the widening income inequality that may arise from differential access to educational opportunities during and after health emergencies.

3 Elements of Health System Preparedness

3.1 Health Systems were Unprepared for COVID-19

Health systems in many economies were unprepared to deal with the COVID-19 pandemic. Health systems need both a national emergency-response strategy and enough resources to function properly when an emergency strikes (WHO 2023). Emergency preparedness requires effective public health infrastructure, communications, and priority-based resource allocation. There must be sufficient surge capacity—in medical personnel, equipment and supplies, hospitals and clinics, and coordinated management within and across various system levels. This largely determines how successful mitigation measures will be in limiting the damage caused by a pandemic. An effective emergency response also requires coordination between central and local authorities—and affected communities—in planning and deploying available medical supplies and health workers. The pandemic highlighted the many challenges governments must overcome in preparing for future health emergencies.

The Global Health Security Index (GHSI) provides a benchmark measure of an economy's health security capacity. The GHSI compares an economy's preparedness to international health regulations (IHR 2005). It assesses an economy's health security across six broad categories of preparedness: prevention, detection, rapid response, health system, compliance with international norms, and risk environment (Bell and Nuzzo 2021). It uses only transparent, available data to measure public health and healthcare preparedness—including cross-cutting factors related to biological threat mitigation, socioeconomic resilience, and societal vulnerabilities. Published a year before COVID-19 hit, the 2019 GHSI was particularly timely as it provided baseline data on preparedness, along with information on the potential risk factors for future health emergency preparedness.

One year into the pandemic, a 2021 update was compiled. The GHSI assigns the highest scores to economies with the most capacity to prevent and respond to epidemics and pandemics (Figure 3.1).

Health security capacity did not improve much a year into the pandemic. In 2021, 91% of economies worldwide did not have a national response plan, program, or guidelines to provide medical countermeasures—such as vaccines and antiviral drugs—to deal with the unprecedented COVID-19 public health emergency (Bell and Nuzzo 2021). Some economies were able to minimize mortality, reducing disease transmission by adapting the strategic preparedness and response plan developed and updated by WHO and its partners (WHO 2021). Those that followed the plan adapted their national responses accordingly to coordinate responses through community engagement, providing laboratory testing facilities and clinical referral systems. However, the GHSI shows that many economies remain dangerously unprepared to fight future epidemics, pandemics, or other health emergencies. The 2021 report concluded that only 20% of 195 economies had invested nationally during the previous 3 years to improve their ability to respond to the threat of an epidemic—only two low-income economies were in the group. Just 25% had published a workforce strategy over the previous 5 years. The majority did not have a well-defined risk communication strategy or published a health emergency response plan for diseases that could develop into an epidemic or pandemic. And most scored less than 50 (out of 100) on health security—which covers government biosecurity systems, training, personnel vetting, transporting infectious substances, and cross-border transfers and screening.

Figure 3.1 Global Health Security Index Overall Scores

Health security capacity varies substantially across the region and did not improve much a year into the pandemic.

Legend:
- 2019
- 2021
- 2019 average
- 2021 average

A. Developing Asia

B. Advanced Economies

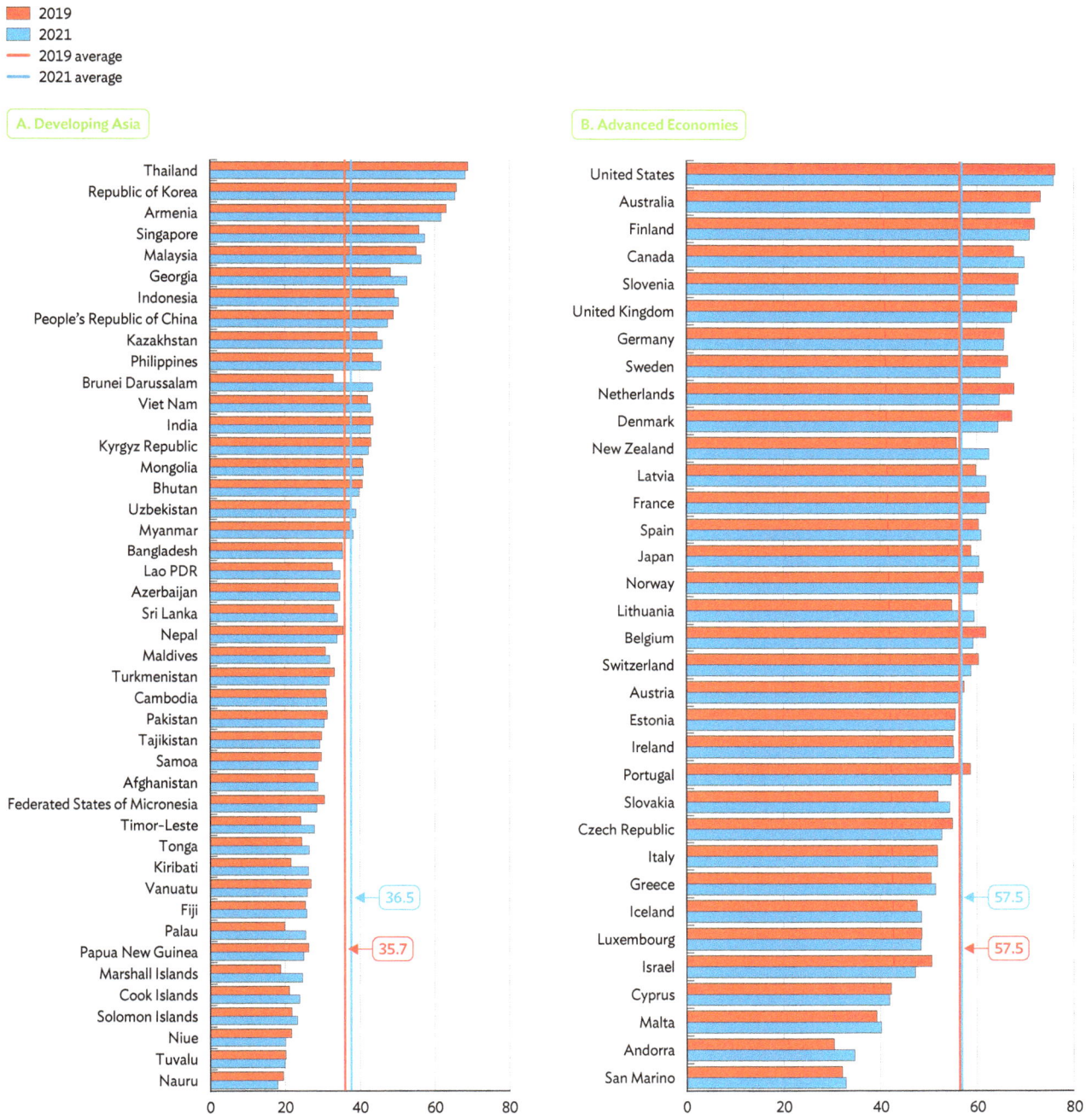

Lao PDR = Lao People's Democratic Republic.

Sources: Global Health Security Index; Bell and Nuzzo 2021.

3.2 Health System Efficiency

Health system preparedness relies on efficiency, which varies by economy. Ahmed et al. (2024) measure the technical efficiency of health systems in 189 economies using pre-COVID-19 data—such as health expenditure per capita, hospital beds per 1,000 people, and medical doctors per 10,000 people—as input variables, and life expectancy at birth along with the infant mortality rate as output variables (Figure 3.2). Before COVID-19, just 32 economies (17%) had efficient health systems, with the remaining 157 lagging behind.[3] There were also considerable variations across economies. High-income and some lower-income economies had higher than average efficiency scores (a mean score of 0.97). In contrast, lower-middle-income economies and those in Sub-Saharan Africa had relatively lower average efficiency scores (mean scores of 0.93 and 0.91, respectively). Also, there were variations in efficiency based on per capita health expenditure—only a few economies had health expenditure per capita greater than $6,000 (a technical efficiency score above 0.99).

The United States, the country with the highest health expenditure per capita ($10,661), had a relatively inefficient health system (score 0.94).

Higher health system efficiency is associated with less COVID-19 damage. Recent studies document health system inefficiency in economies across the world. Many, including high-income economies, faced enormous challenges in COVID-19 preparedness and outcomes (Lupu and Tiganasu 2022). Economies with a higher technical efficiency tend to perform better in vaccination coverage and had lower excess deaths during 2021–2022. In short, those with relatively efficient health systems better managed the pandemic and saved more lives. Ahmed et al. (2024) show that highly efficient economies were better in testing and tracing COVID-19 cases. They thus recorded relatively higher average number of cases and official COVID-19 deaths per million population (a median of 167,074) than economies with low efficiency scores (93,087). More efficient economies also tended to record higher vaccination coverage (66.1% of the population) than low-efficient economies (54.8%).

Figure 3.2 Health System Technical Efficiency Scores by Income Level Pre-COVID-19

Richer economies tend to have better healthcare system efficiency.

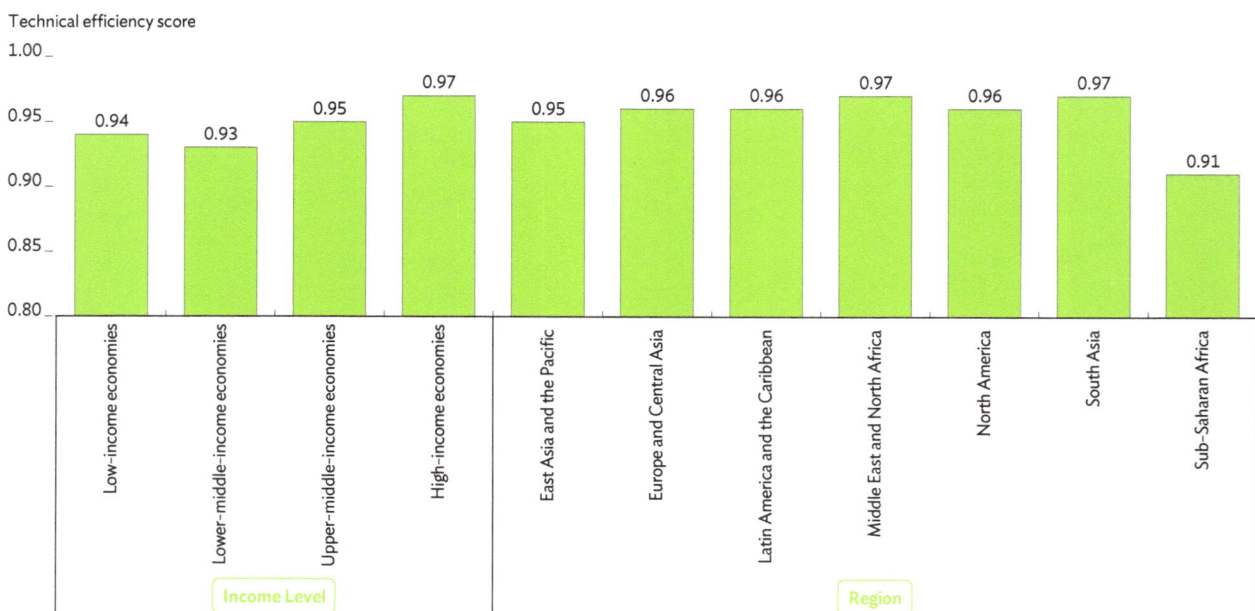

Technical efficiency score

Category	Score
Low-income economies	0.94
Lower-middle-income economies	0.93
Upper-middle-income economies	0.95
High-income economies	0.97
East Asia and the Pacific	0.95
Europe and Central Asia	0.96
Latin America and the Caribbean	0.96
Middle East and North Africa	0.97
North America	0.96
South Asia	0.97
Sub-Saharan Africa	0.91

Income Level | Region

Source: Ahmed et al. 2024.

---

[3]   Economies with a technical efficiency score >0.99 are considered to have an efficient health system (Ahmed et al. 2024).

Figure 3.3 COVID-19 Outcomes and Health System Efficiency

Higher level of efficiency allows for better identification and treatment, fewer excess and total deaths, and better vaccination outcomes.

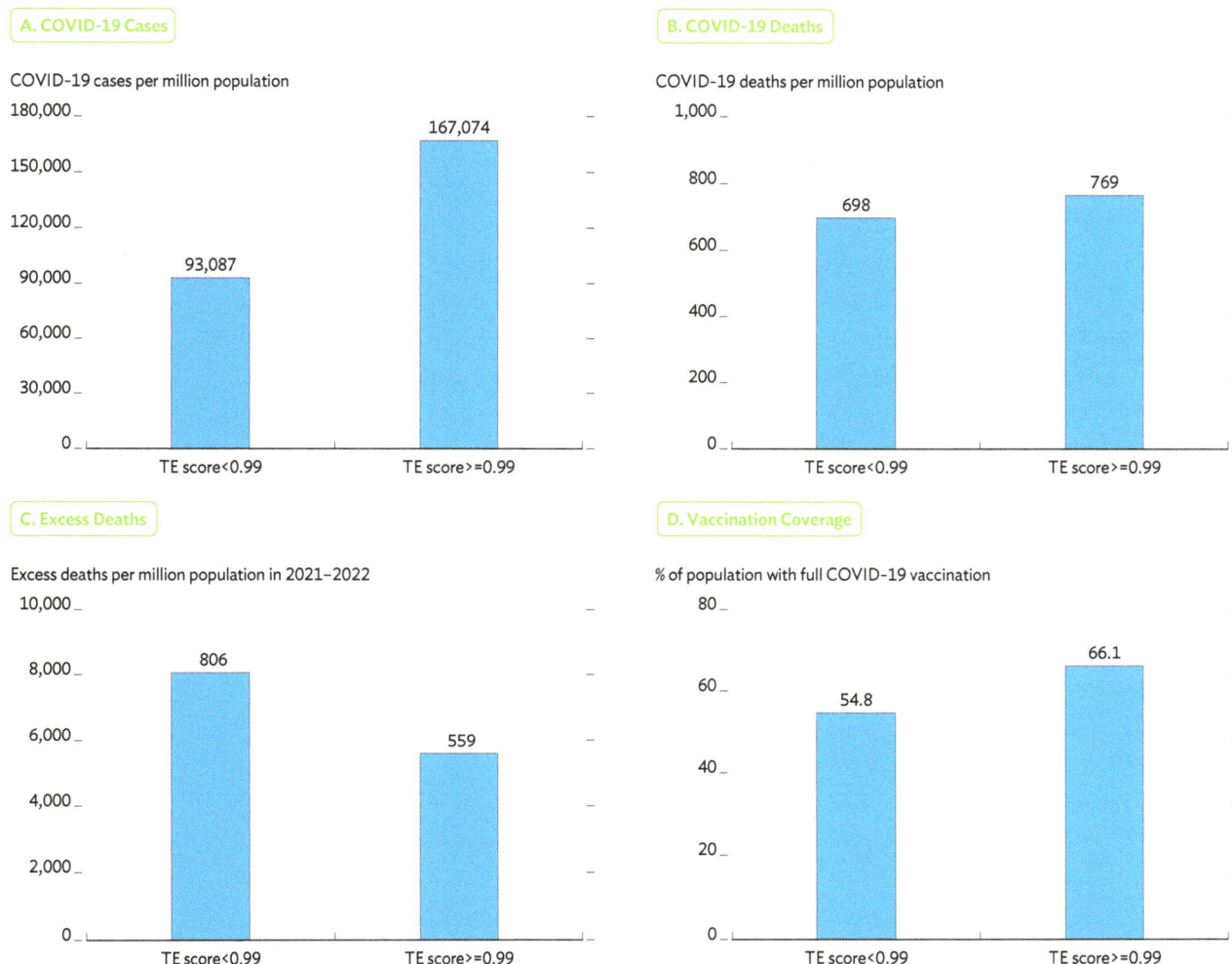

A. COVID-19 Cases

COVID-19 cases per million population

- 93,087 (TE score<0.99)
- 167,074 (TE score>=0.99)

B. COVID-19 Deaths

COVID-19 deaths per million population

- 698 (TE score<0.99)
- 769 (TE score>=0.99)

C. Excess Deaths

Excess deaths per million population in 2021–2022

- 806 (TE score<0.99)
- 559 (TE score>=0.99)

D. Vaccination Coverage

% of population with full COVID-19 vaccination

- 54.8 (TE score<0.99)
- 66.1 (TE score>=0.99)

Excess deaths = COVID-19 deaths + deaths indirectly associated with COVID-19 (such as impact on health systems and behavior changes) – deaths under normal circumstances, TE = technical efficiency.
Source: Ahmed et al. 2024.

As a result, the average excess mortality during the pandemic was lower in highly efficient economies (a median of 559 per million population) than in less efficient ones (806). However, with the data relatively noisy, standard deviations of these COVID-19 outcome indicators were high across economies (Figure 3.3).

Healthcare infrastructure is critical to health system efficiency and health emergency preparedness. Health infrastructure across Asia and the Pacific varies widely. Sy et al. (2024) measure healthcare infrastructure, such as hospital density, available clinics, laboratories, and hospital beds,

including those in intensive care units (ICUs) (Figure 3.4). Prior to COVID-19, there were an average 0.29 hospitals per 10,000 population, 0.22 clinics per 10,000 population, and 0.05 labs per 100,000 population. The Republic of Korea, Timor-Leste, and Japan had the highest hospital density, whereas Georgia had the highest density of medical laboratories. Pressures on the availability of hospitals per population is high in South Asia. The number of hospital and ICU beds per 10,000 population in the Republic of Korea; Kazakhstan; and Taipei,China are higher than in Southeast and South Asia (Figure 3.5).

Figure 3.4 Health Infrastructure in Asia and the Pacific, 2023

The availability of health infrastructure varies across Asia.

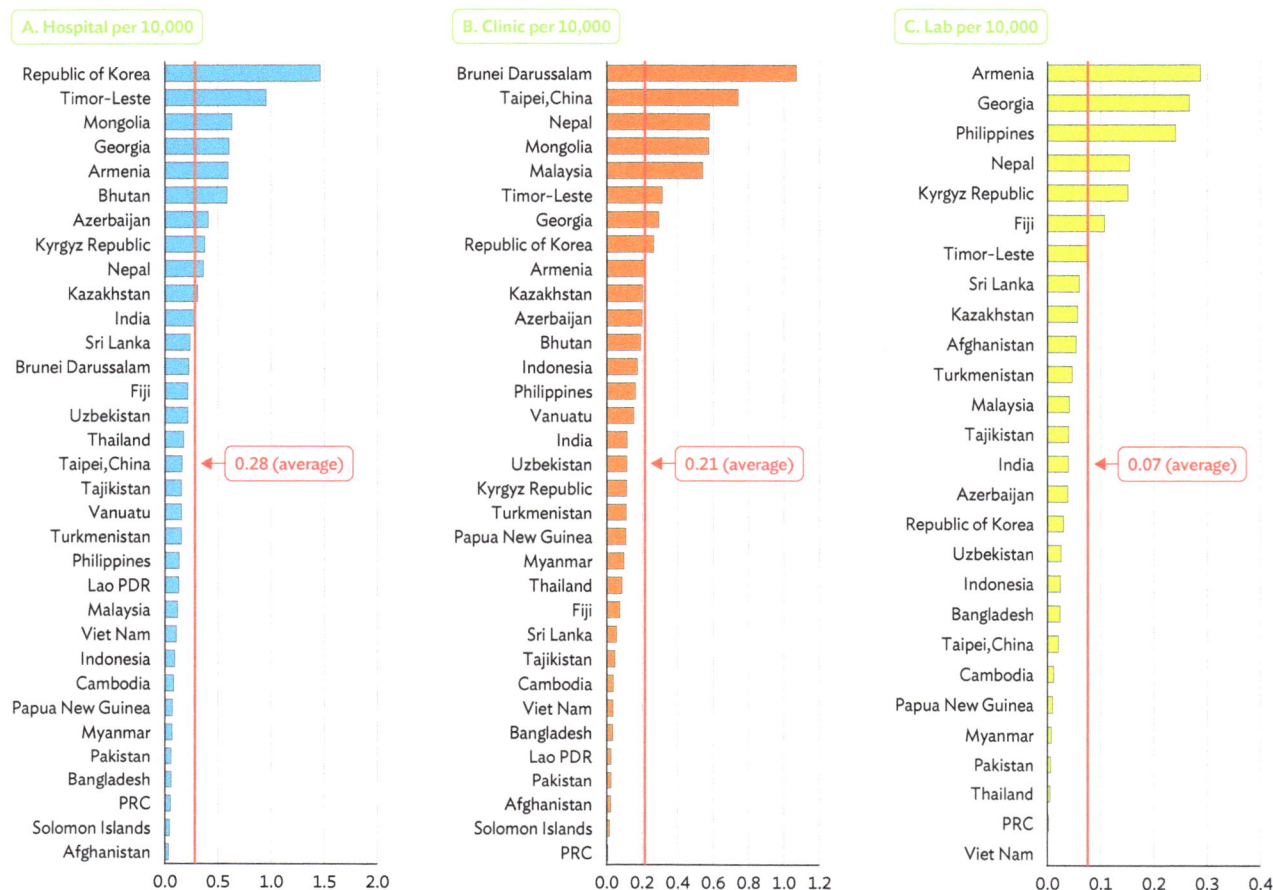

Lao PDR = Lao People's Democratic Republic, PRC = People's Republic of China.

Note: Includes economies with available data.

Source: Sy et al. 2024, based on OpenStreetMaps.

ICU bed utilization also differed substantially, with Bangladesh and Pakistan unable to meet demand. By contrast, Taipei,China; the Republic of Korea; and the People's Republic of China (PRC) had the lowest average ICU bed utilization (Figure 3.6).

A shortage of healthcare workers significantly compromised health system efficiency.
According to the 2021 GHSI report, only 49 economies have published an updated health workforce strategy with plans to overcome health worker shortages across different fields (Bell and Nuzzo 2021). In Asia, 2019 data show an average of 14.5 physicians per 10,000 population, 42.8 nursing and midwifery personnel per 10,000 population, and 27.5 medical lab technicians per 100,000 population.

However, the distribution across economies varies widely. In physicians per 10,000 population, Georgia, Azerbaijan, and Armenia have the most (Figure 3.7). Uzbekistan, Azerbaijan, and Kazakhstan rank at the top in nurses and midwives personnel per 10,000 population, while Singapore; Taipei,China; and the PRC are highest in medical technicians per 100,000 population.

3.3 Surge Capacity

Most governments were surprised by the level of surge capacity required to adequately respond to COVID-19. The pandemic overwhelmed both designated health services and existing surge capacity.

Figure 3.5 Hospital Bed Density in Asia and the Pacific, 2019

The availability of hospital beds also varies widely.

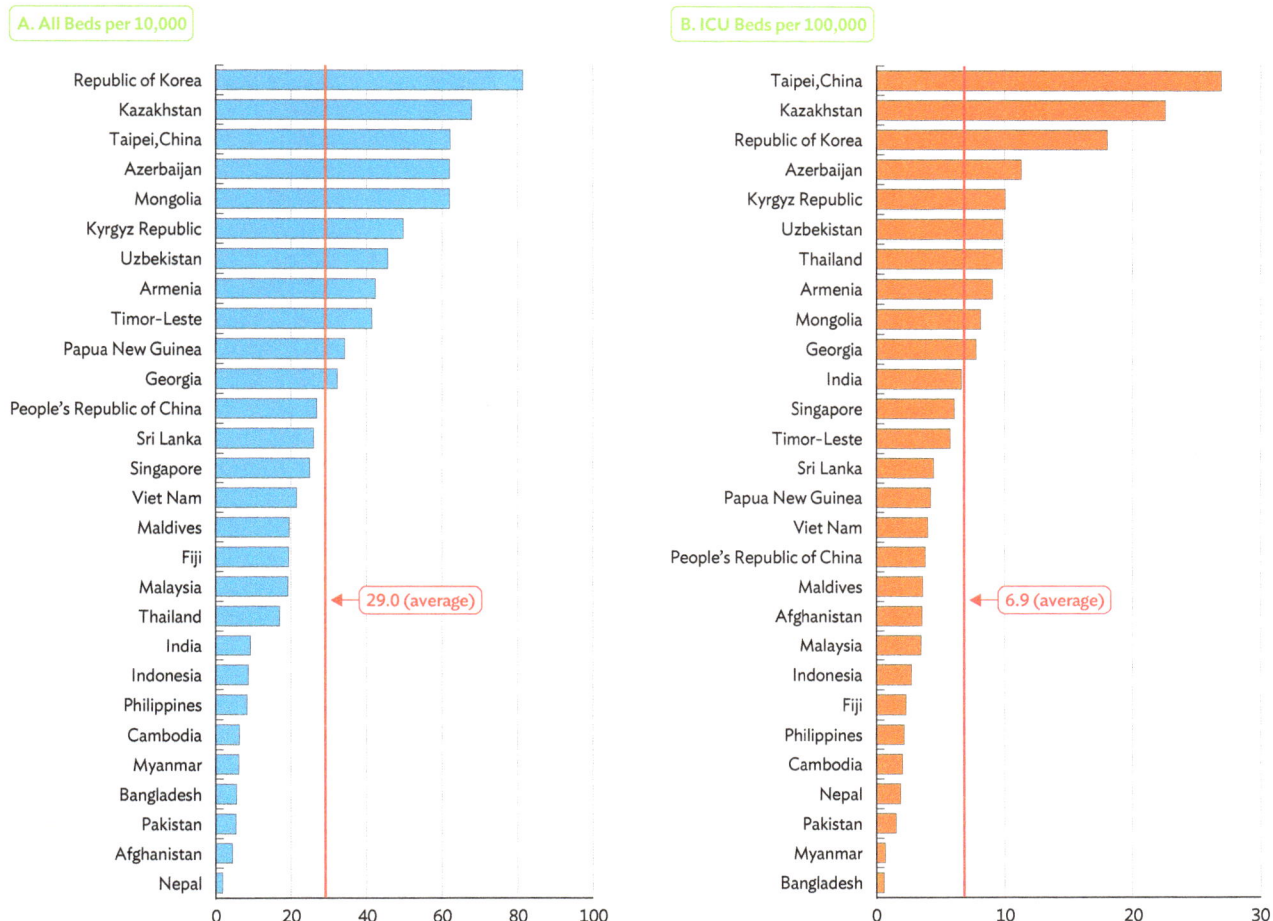

A. All Beds per 10,000

B. ICU Beds per 100,000

ICU = intensive care unit.

Note: Includes economies with available data.

Source: Sy et al. 2024, based on Global Health Data Exchange estimates.

Many economies saw how fragile their health systems were—characterized by poor healthcare infrastructure, greater inequality, inefficiency, and lack of human resources (WHO 2023). In many economies, hospitals were forced to operate well above capacity, with many calling up retired employees, students, and military personnel to support their health workforce. In some cases, emergency funds were used to hire new healthcare workers. Temporary staffing plans had to consider each individual's training and relevant experience, as most normally worked in non-medical jobs (WHO 2023). Regulations had to be adjusted to hire new healthcare personnel—extending or simply creating the required licenses or certifications.

Some economies addressed their health system limitations better than others. Germany, the PRC, and the Republic of Korea dealt with the surge well. Based on early epidemiological forecasts, Germany expanded its ICU capacity from 28,000 beds to 40,000 beds equipped with ventilators. The PRC installed two modular hospitals in Wuhan and added 2,500 beds in less than 2 weeks. The Republic of Korea reserved hospital beds for severe COVID-19 patients, keeping milder cases in dormitories that provided universal free access. Thailand leveraged its network of over one million community workers to help prevent, detect, and report cases (Osewe 2021).

Figure 3.6 Hospital Bed and ICU Utilization in Asia and the Pacific

Most and least heavily pressured hospitals in Asia during COVID-19.

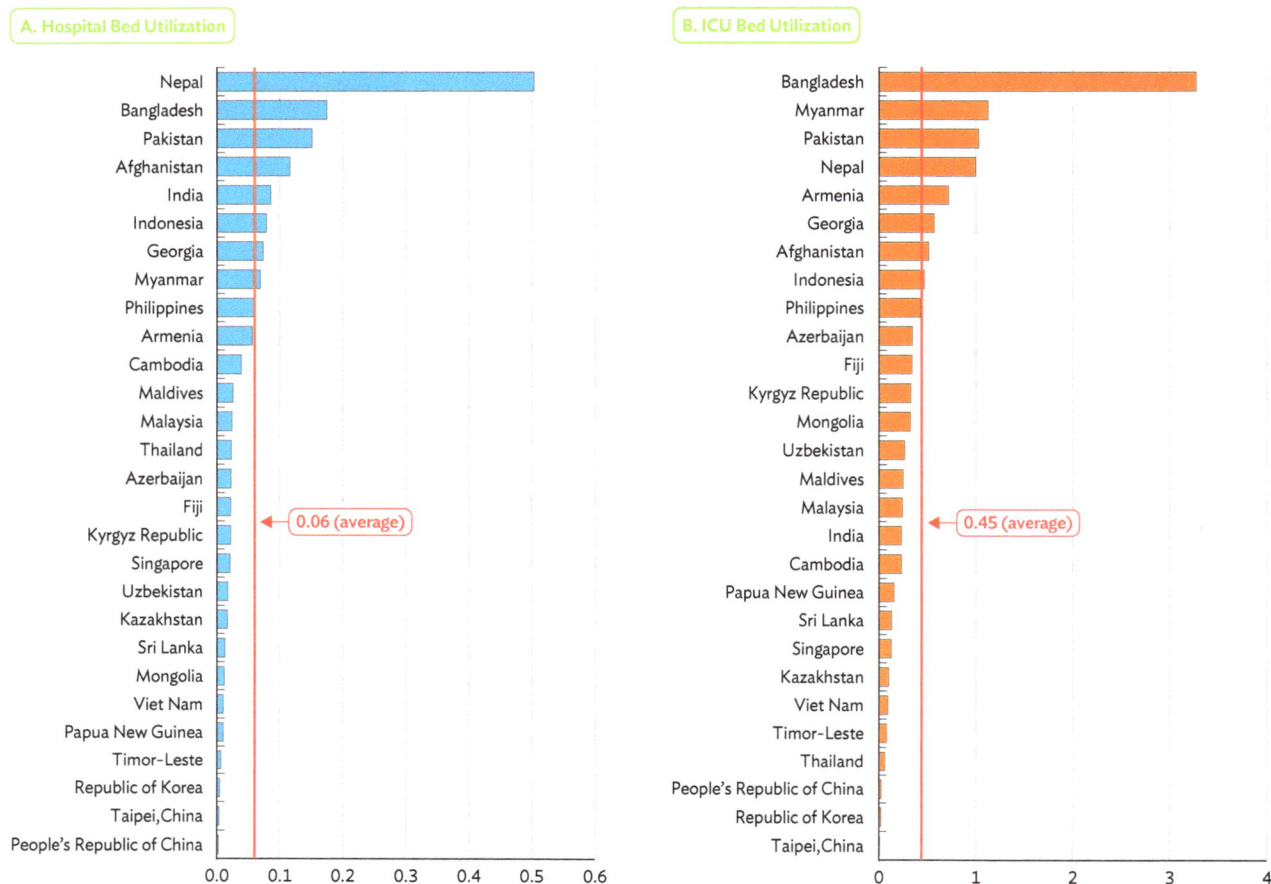

A. Hospital Bed Utilization

0.06 (average)

B. ICU Bed Utilization

0.45 (average)

ICU = intensive care unit.
Note: Includes economies with available data.
Source: Sy et al. 2024.

Initiatives that boost clinical capacity for future emergencies require smooth coordination between the government, private institutions, as well as non-government and international organizations to ensure healthcare facilities are not overwhelmed (WHO 2023).

India's experience in managing surge capacity offers insight from a developing economy's perspective. Bhatia (2024) documents how India used the government's three-tier system of health facilities to better manage COVID-19 cases. It includes (i) care centers with isolation beds for mild or symptomatic cases, (ii) dedicated health facilities with oxygen-supported isolation beds for moderate cases, and (iii) dedicated hospitals with

ICU beds for severe cases. By the end of 2020, the government had installed 15,378 treatment facilities with nearly 1.3 million isolation beds, 270,710 oxygen-supported isolation beds, and 81,113 (40,627) ICU (ventilator-ICU) beds. The government also repurposed industrial oxygen for medical use to boost supply for COVID-19 patients—installing oxygen plants in hospitals and transporting liquid medical oxygen via special flights and trains throughout the country. At the beginning of the pandemic, the government trained many healthcare professionals using its Integrated Government Online Training platform (iGOT). From the start of the pandemic until December 2021, about 1.4 million unique users registered on iGOT, with 8 million additional health workers trained through state governments.

Figure 3.7 Healthcare Workforce Density in Asia and the Pacific, 2019

Distribution of healthcare workers varies widely across the region.

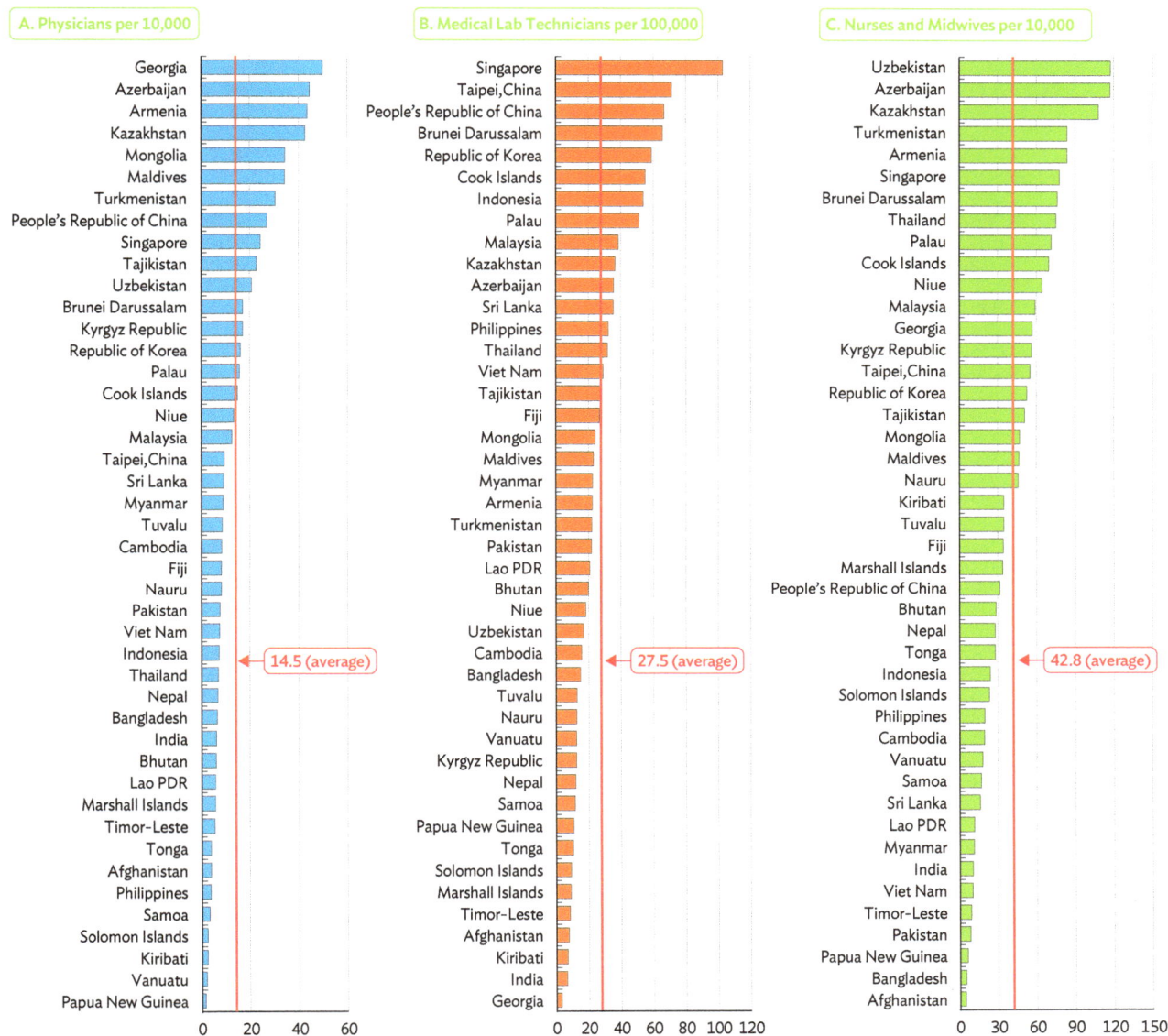

A. Physicians per 10,000	B. Medical Lab Technicians per 100,000	C. Nurses and Midwives per 10,000
Georgia	Singapore	Uzbekistan
Azerbaijan	Taipei,China	Azerbaijan
Armenia	People's Republic of China	Kazakhstan
Kazakhstan	Brunei Darussalam	Turkmenistan
Mongolia	Republic of Korea	Armenia
Maldives	Cook Islands	Singapore
Turkmenistan	Indonesia	Brunei Darussalam
People's Republic of China	Palau	Thailand
Singapore	Malaysia	Palau
Tajikistan	Kazakhstan	Cook Islands
Uzbekistan	Azerbaijan	Niue
Brunei Darussalam	Sri Lanka	Malaysia
Kyrgyz Republic	Philippines	Georgia
Republic of Korea	Thailand	Kyrgyz Republic
Palau	Viet Nam	Taipei,China
Cook Islands	Tajikistan	Republic of Korea
Niue	Fiji	Tajikistan
Malaysia	Mongolia	Mongolia
Taipei,China	Maldives	Maldives
Sri Lanka	Myanmar	Nauru
Myanmar	Armenia	Kiribati
Tuvalu	Turkmenistan	Tuvalu
Cambodia	Pakistan	Fiji
Fiji	Lao PDR	Marshall Islands
Nauru	Bhutan	People's Republic of China
Pakistan	Niue	Bhutan
Viet Nam	Uzbekistan	Nepal
Indonesia — 14.5 (average)	Cambodia	Tonga
Thailand	Bangladesh — 27.5 (average)	Indonesia — 42.8 (average)
Nepal	Tuvalu	Solomon Islands
Bangladesh	Nauru	Philippines
India	Vanuatu	Cambodia
Bhutan	Kyrgyz Republic	Vanuatu
Lao PDR	Nepal	Samoa
Marshall Islands	Samoa	Sri Lanka
Timor-Leste	Papua New Guinea	Lao PDR
Tonga	Tonga	Myanmar
Afghanistan	Solomon Islands	India
Philippines	Marshall Islands	Viet Nam
Samoa	Timor-Leste	Timor-Leste
Solomon Islands	Afghanistan	Pakistan
Kiribati	Kiribati	Papua New Guinea
Vanuatu	India	Bangladesh
Papua New Guinea	Georgia	Afghanistan
0 20 40 60	0 20 40 60 80 100 120	0 30 60 90 120 150

Lao PDR = Lao People's Democratic Republic.

Note: Includes economies with available data.

Source: Sy et al. 2024, based on Global Health Data Exchange estimates.

3.4 Primary Health System

During emergencies, primary health facilities can serve non-critical patients. Good primary healthcare improves overall health, reduces co-morbidity risks, and is the first line of defense during health emergencies. It provides primary care, but also serves as a reliable information hub. It effectively supports core public health functions like surveillance, outbreak management, delivers countermeasures, and builds trust among citizens, which is critical for emergency management. A well-equipped facility with trained personnel reduces the burden of secondary and tertiary health facilities, allowing the latter to focus on the most critical patients, those directly affected by the emergency or others. Integrated health systems can centralize patient demand management, available resources, and care facilities. Economies had to coordinate COVID-19 and non-COVID-19 facilities, concentrating clinical resources to COVID-19 patients while maintaining essential services in other facilities (Yang et al. 2021; MacGregor et al. 2022; WHO 2023).

Combined with telemedicine, primary health systems can adequately treat all patients with mild symptoms. In combination, the two significantly increased surge capacity. Many health systems set up dedicated testing clinics and follow-up arrangements so severely infected patients received immediate care, while mild patients were treated at home or as outpatients with the help of telemedicine where available. For example, Germany's investment in telemedicine helped immensely during the pandemic in satisfying patient needs (Yoo et al. 2021). Hungary, Ireland, and Malta used dedicated phone lines for consultations on caller symptoms, sending suspected cases for clinical testing. The Indonesian government created its own mobile application and partnered with telemedicine operators to treat mild cases. It also broadcasted or otherwise spread information on COVID-19 preventive actions, and even scheduled vaccinations (Nur Aisyah et al. 2023).

3.5 Medical Countermeasures

Medical countermeasures (MCMs) are the lynchpin of pandemic preparedness and response. MCMs refer to both pharmaceutical and non-pharmaceutical products, including vaccines, therapeutics, diagnostic tools, and personal protective equipment. They reduce additional strain on the health system, protect people at risk, and potentially save lives. According to the 2021 GHSI (Bell and Nuzzo 2021), 73% of economies worldwide do not provide fast-track approval for producing MCMs during emergencies. The technological and innovation capacities for manufacturing and distributing MCMs vary greatly between economies and are concentrated in only a few economies. Manufacturing capacity for MCMs and other tools domestically or regionally allows for easy and timely access to supply chains in an emergency (WHO 2023). A legal and regulatory framework should be in place to conduct clinical trials and authorize

MCM use during health emergencies. Most economies also need either quick access to direct funding or through regional mechanisms—including procurement and distribution—to ensure adequate international MCM supply. Additional funds and frameworks are needed to support community mobilization. Global and domestic coordination platforms are also needed for equitable and effective access to MCMs.

Developing effective vaccines quickly is challenging during a pandemic. Scientists were able to develop safe and effective vaccines much faster than during previous emergencies, producing a variety of safe and effective vaccines that helped contain COVID-19 transmission. The reasons vaccines were so rapidly developed and deployed included (i) the huge financial investments in research and development accompanied by advance purchase agreements, (ii) demand by governments and international agencies, (iii) previous scientific research and innovations on vaccine platform technologies (such as mRNA), and (iv) accelerated clinical development along with regulatory reviews and approvals (Excler et al. 2023). As of July 2023, 65% of the world's population had been vaccinated, receiving all shots prescribed by the initial vaccination protocol (OWID 2023). However, it remains uncertain whether developing such rapid and effective vaccines for a future pathogen pandemic would be possible. Innovations in advanced market commitment could help (Kremer 2023).

Inequitable access to vaccines became a problem. The availability of vaccines varied greatly by economy (Tabuga 2024). Data from the International Monetary Fund-WHO COVID-19 Vaccine Tracker show the disparities by access and secured doses (Figure 3.8). Vaccines obtained by some economies were as much as 8 to 10 times their population (for example, Australia, Switzerland, and Canada). Among ADB developing members, availability ranged from less than two in Papua New Guinea to more than four in Cambodia. While some economies made bilateral deals to obtain vaccines, there were wide disparities between developing/least developed economies and high-income economies (Tabuga 2024) (Figure 3.9). Some early "deals" were for largely untested vaccines. In addition, there were external supply restrictions as well as internal distribution bottlenecks that limited vaccine access to the wider population in many low-income economies.

Figure 3.8 Secured and/or Expected Vaccines as a Multiple of Population

Vaccines distributed unequally across the globe.

■ Developing Asia   ■ Others

A. High-income Economies

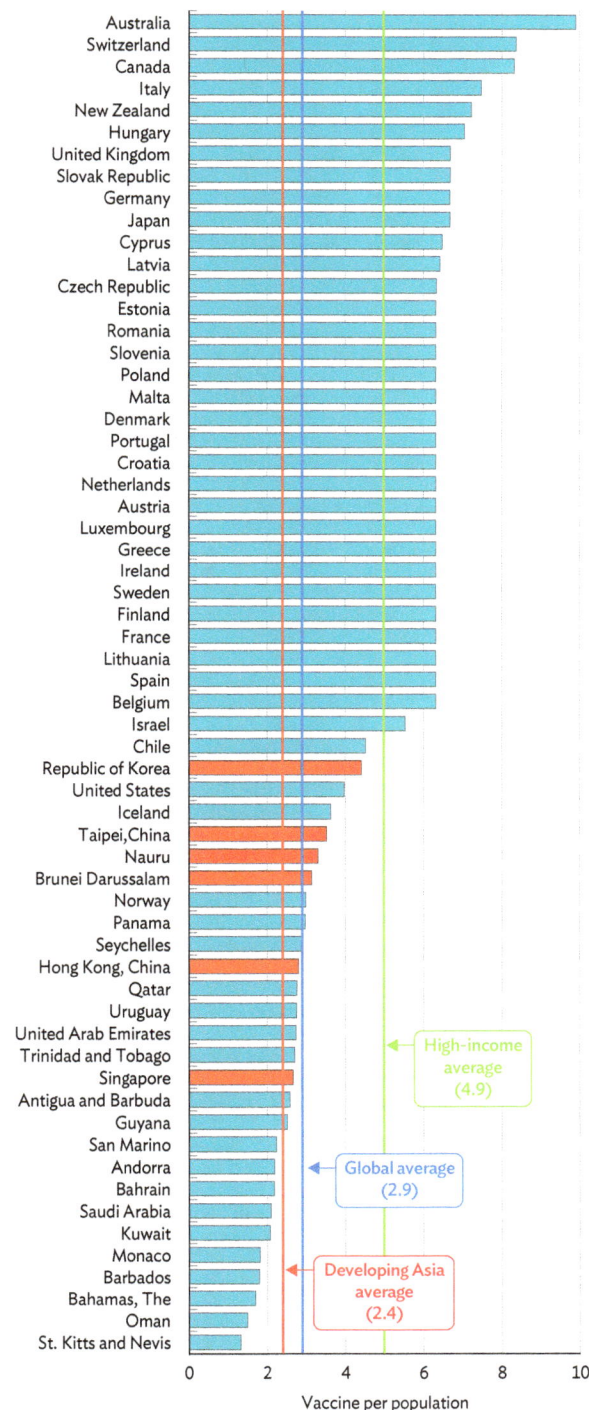

Australia, Switzerland, Canada, Italy, New Zealand, Hungary, United Kingdom, Slovak Republic, Germany, Japan, Cyprus, Latvia, Czech Republic, Estonia, Romania, Slovenia, Poland, Malta, Denmark, Portugal, Croatia, Netherlands, Austria, Luxembourg, Greece, Ireland, Sweden, Finland, France, Lithuania, Spain, Belgium, Israel, Chile, Republic of Korea, United States, Iceland, Taipei,China, Nauru, Brunei Darussalam, Norway, Panama, Seychelles, Hong Kong, China, Qatar, Uruguay, United Arab Emirates, Trinidad and Tobago, Singapore, Antigua and Barbuda, Guyana, San Marino, Andorra, Bahrain, Saudi Arabia, Kuwait, Monaco, Barbados, Bahamas, The, Oman, St. Kitts and Nevis

High-income average (4.9)
Global average (2.9)
Developing Asia average (2.4)

Vaccine per population

B. Upper-middle-income Economies

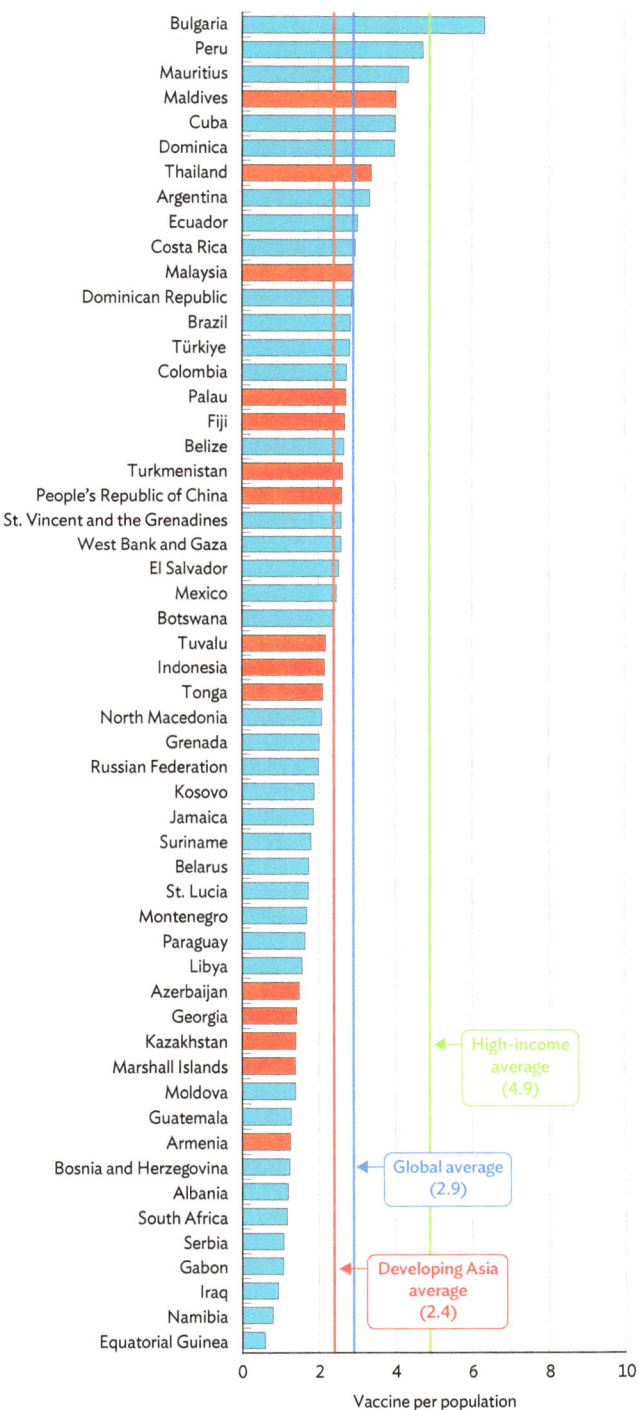

Bulgaria, Peru, Mauritius, Maldives, Cuba, Dominica, Thailand, Argentina, Ecuador, Costa Rica, Malaysia, Dominican Republic, Brazil, Türkiye, Colombia, Palau, Fiji, Belize, Turkmenistan, People's Republic of China, St. Vincent and the Grenadines, West Bank and Gaza, El Salvador, Mexico, Botswana, Tuvalu, Indonesia, Tonga, North Macedonia, Grenada, Russian Federation, Kosovo, Jamaica, Suriname, Belarus, St. Lucia, Montenegro, Paraguay, Libya, Azerbaijan, Georgia, Kazakhstan, Marshall Islands, Moldova, Guatemala, Armenia, Bosnia and Herzegovina, Albania, South Africa, Serbia, Gabon, Iraq, Namibia, Equatorial Guinea

High-income average (4.9)
Global average (2.9)
Developing Asia average (2.4)

Vaccine per population

continued on next page

Figure 3.8 *Continued*

■ Developing Asia   ■ Others

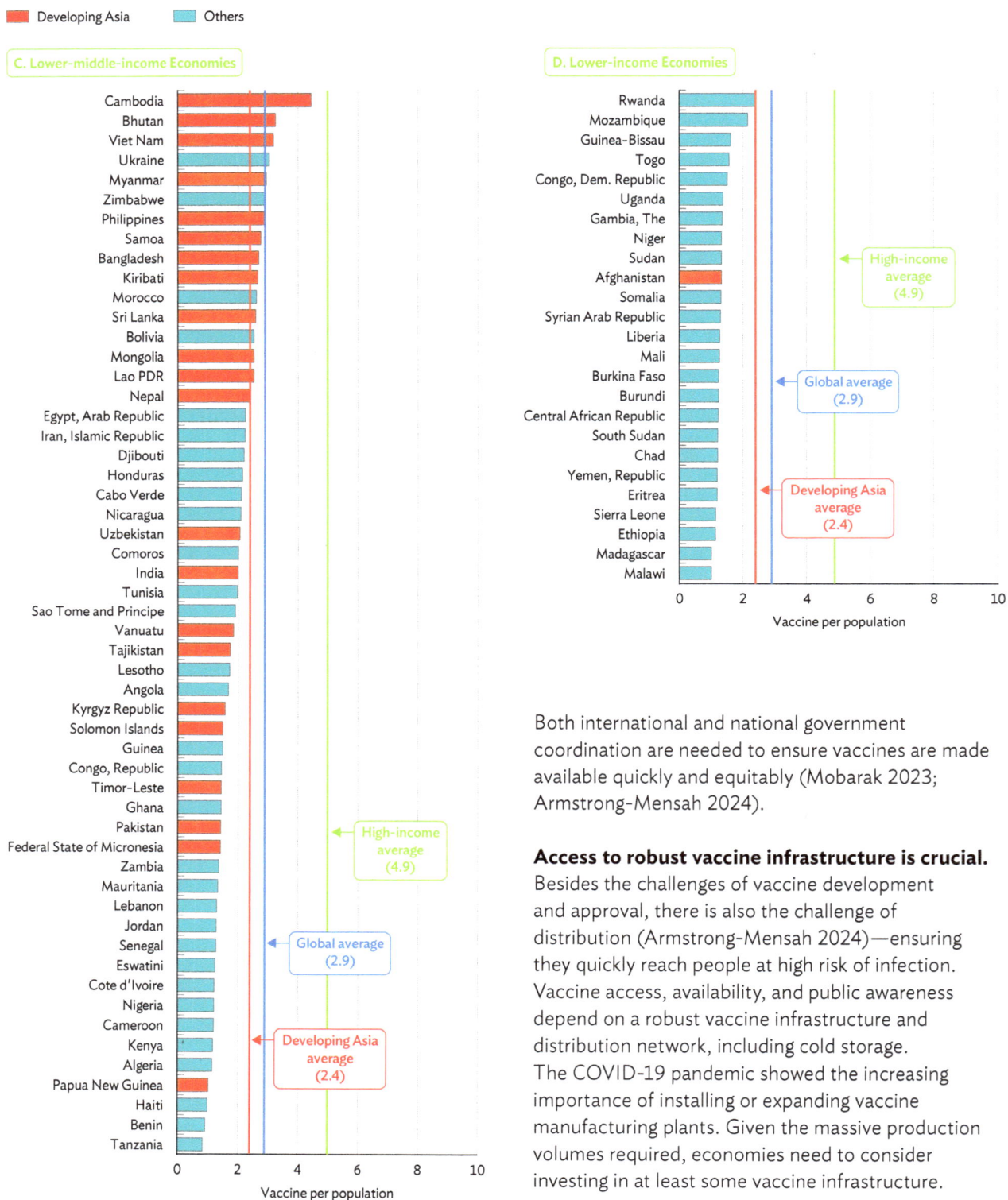

C. Lower-middle-income Economies

Cambodia, Bhutan, Viet Nam, Ukraine, Myanmar, Zimbabwe, Philippines, Samoa, Bangladesh, Kiribati, Morocco, Sri Lanka, Bolivia, Mongolia, Lao PDR, Nepal, Egypt, Arab Republic, Iran, Islamic Republic, Djibouti, Honduras, Cabo Verde, Nicaragua, Uzbekistan, Comoros, India, Tunisia, Sao Tome and Principe, Vanuatu, Tajikistan, Lesotho, Angola, Kyrgyz Republic, Solomon Islands, Guinea, Congo, Republic, Timor-Leste, Ghana, Pakistan, Federal State of Micronesia, Zambia, Mauritania, Lebanon, Jordan, Senegal, Eswatini, Cote d'Ivoire, Nigeria, Cameroon, Kenya, Algeria, Papua New Guinea, Haiti, Benin, Tanzania

High-income average (4.9)
Global average (2.9)
Developing Asia average (2.4)

Vaccine per population

D. Lower-income Economies

Rwanda, Mozambique, Guinea-Bissau, Togo, Congo, Dem. Republic, Uganda, Gambia, The, Niger, Sudan, Afghanistan, Somalia, Syrian Arab Republic, Liberia, Mali, Burkina Faso, Burundi, Central African Republic, South Sudan, Chad, Yemen, Republic, Eritrea, Sierra Leone, Ethiopia, Madagascar, Malawi

High-income average (4.9)
Global average (2.9)
Developing Asia average (2.4)

Vaccine per population

Both international and national government coordination are needed to ensure vaccines are made available quickly and equitably (Mobarak 2023; Armstrong-Mensah 2024).

Access to robust vaccine infrastructure is crucial.
Besides the challenges of vaccine development and approval, there is also the challenge of distribution (Armstrong-Mensah 2024)—ensuring they quickly reach people at high risk of infection. Vaccine access, availability, and public awareness depend on a robust vaccine infrastructure and distribution network, including cold storage. The COVID-19 pandemic showed the increasing importance of installing or expanding vaccine manufacturing plants. Given the massive production volumes required, economies need to consider investing in at least some vaccine infrastructure.

Lao PDR = Lao People's Democratic Republic.
Sources: IMF-WHO COVID-19 Vaccine Tracker, updated 31 August 2022; Tabuga 2024.

Figure 3.9 Deal/Report Date of Initial Bilateral Deals for Vaccine Supply, Number of Days since WHO Classified COVID-19 as a Pandemic

Access to procure vaccines varied widely across economies.

Although higher-income economies should naturally invest in more capacity for potential vaccines, they should be based on a careful economic cost-benefit analysis. All economies should "invest at risk"—investing early by carefully calculating the potential socio-economic benefits net of costs, which include adjustments from possible investment failures. Thus, governments would likely have to spearhead investments, with the optimal investment program differing across economies (Kremer 2023).

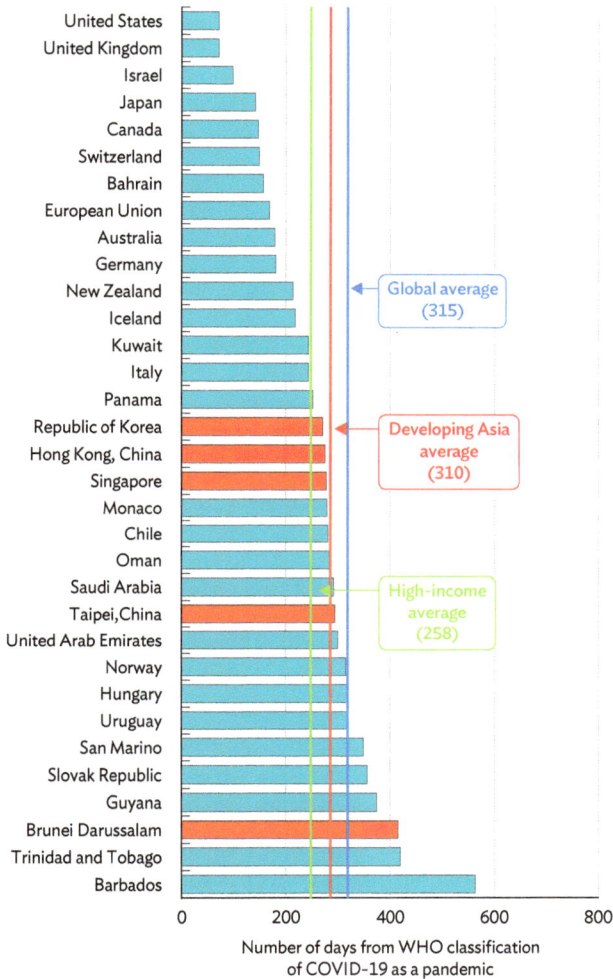

Investments that boost vaccine supply chain capacity are needed as well. In addition to high vaccine development costs, investments need to develop human resources, data management, and the distribution network (OECD 2021).

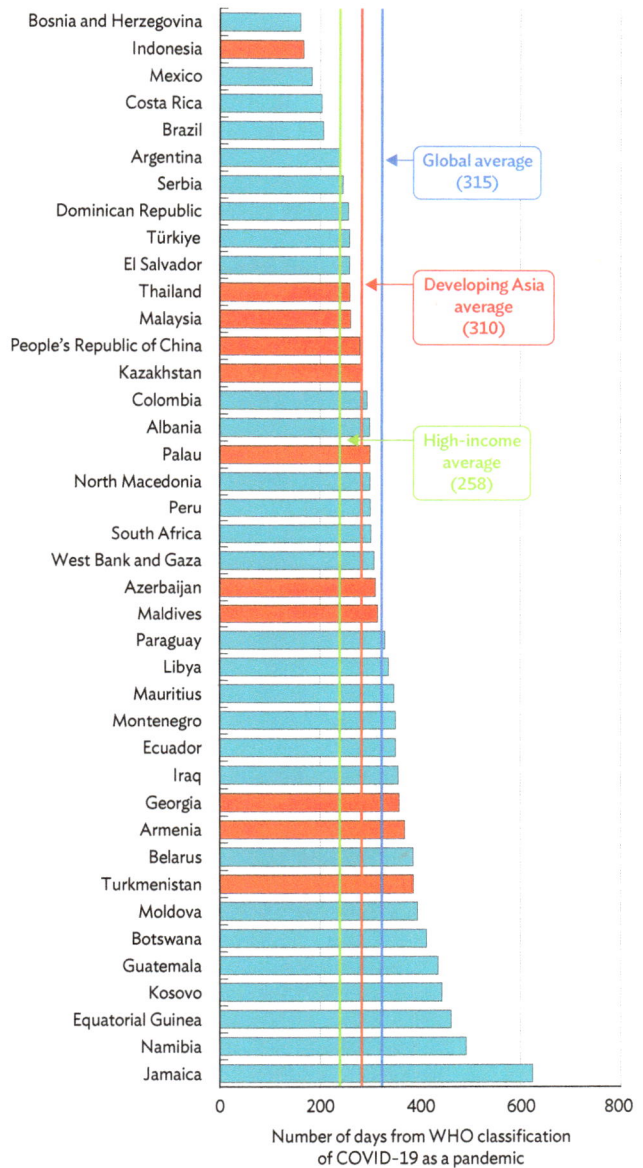

continued on next page

Figure 3.9 *Continued*

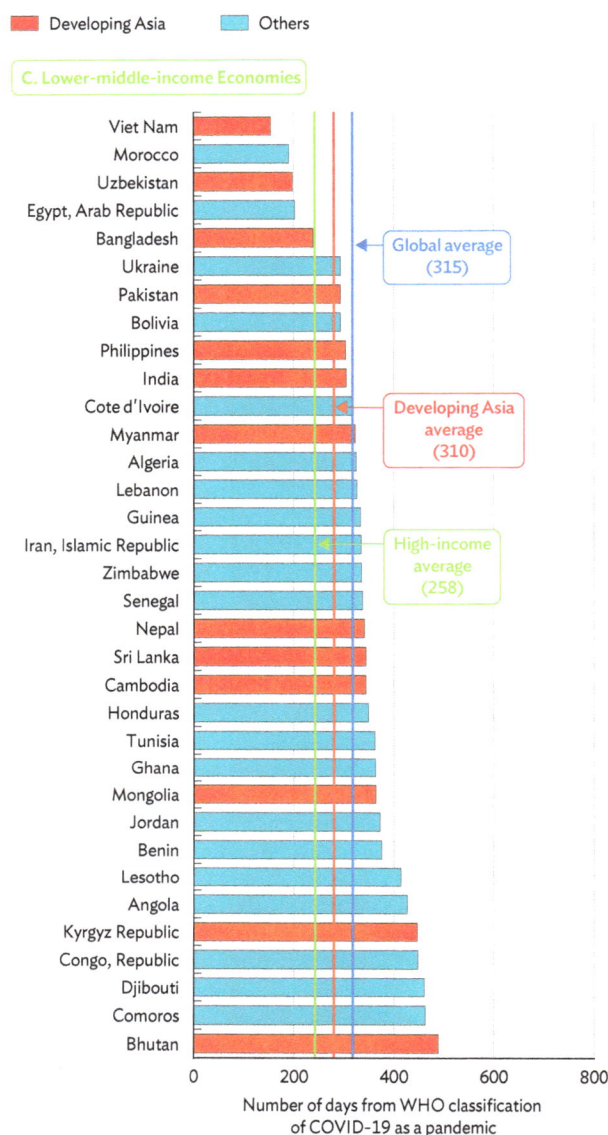

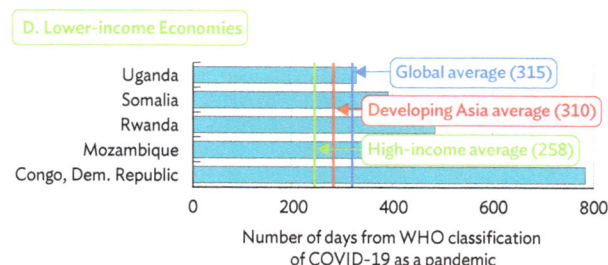

■ Developing Asia   ■ Others

C. Lower-middle-income Economies

Number of days from WHO classification
of COVID-19 as a pandemic

D. Lower-income Economies

Number of days from WHO classification
of COVID-19 as a pandemic

Lao PDR = Lao People's Democratic Republic, WHO = World Health Organization.

Sources: IMF-WHO COVID-19 Vaccine Tracker (updated 31 August 2022); Tabuga 2024.

An effective and equitable global arrangement will be crucial as not all economies can invest in vaccine manufacturing. Upfront finance is needed to buy and deliver vaccines (Kremer 2023). During the pandemic, global and regional alliances—along with support from multilateral development agencies—proved crucial for both. Development partners can provide support for early investments in vaccine procurement. And they can offer support in structuring contracts in addition to providing financial support. Moreover, as some economies build new vaccine manufacturing and distribution infrastructure, sustaining those initiatives will require innovative planning and investment.

3.6 Health System Funding

Health emergency preparedness requires long-term financial investment. The challenge lies in investing adequately in pandemic preparedness, including core public health functions such as surveillance and rapid response, coordination and communications, and delivery of essential care. Per capita spending on health, government health budgets as a percent of total allocations, as well as out of pocket expenditures vary greatly across economies. Among ADB developing members, public spending on health in 2020 ranged from 0.5% of GDP in Bangladesh to nearly 20% of GDP in Tuvalu as opposed to total health expenditure, which is 2.6% of GDP in Bangladesh and 21.5% of GDP in Tuvalu (Figure 3.10). In 15 economies, many of those low- or low-middle income, more is spent on private investment than public investment. That gap needs to close. For example, while Pacific economies rely significantly on external funding, other low- and lower-middle-income economies in Asia do not.

International efforts must help strengthen the ability of governments to fund pandemic preparedness. The need for health-related development assistance has grown for global public goods such as infectious disease tracking and emerging pathogen detection systems. There are huge disparities in health spending across the world. Although development assistance for pandemic preparedness rose in 2020 and 2021, allocations for health-related responses remained far below recommended targets (Global Burden of Disease 2021 Health Financing Collaborator Network 2023).

Figure 3.10 Nominal Health Expenditure, 2020

A large gap exists in the level and sources of health spending among ADB developing members.

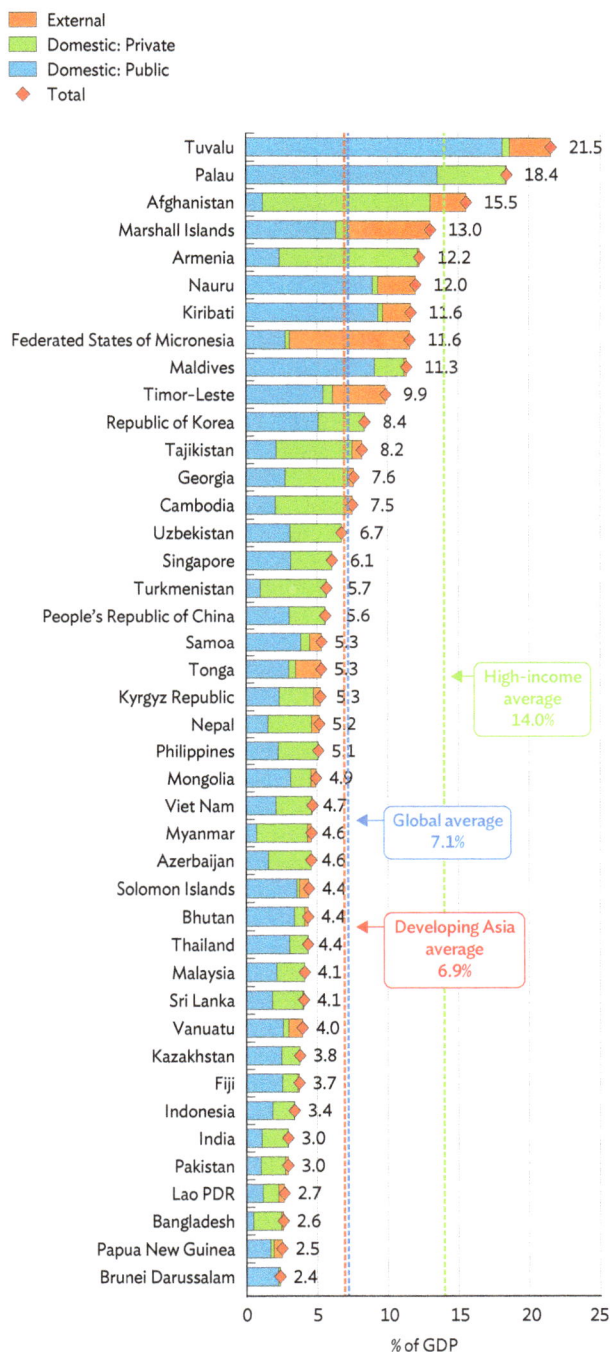

Legend:
- External
- Domestic: Private
- Domestic: Public
- Total

Economy	% of GDP
Tuvalu	21.5
Palau	18.4
Afghanistan	15.5
Marshall Islands	13.0
Armenia	12.2
Nauru	12.0
Kiribati	11.6
Federated States of Micronesia	11.6
Maldives	11.3
Timor-Leste	9.9
Republic of Korea	8.4
Tajikistan	8.2
Georgia	7.6
Cambodia	7.5
Uzbekistan	6.7
Singapore	6.1
Turkmenistan	5.7
People's Republic of China	5.6
Samoa	5.3
Tonga	5.3
Kyrgyz Republic	5.3
Nepal	5.2
Philippines	5.1
Mongolia	4.9
Viet Nam	4.7
Myanmar	4.6
Azerbaijan	4.6
Solomon Islands	4.4
Bhutan	4.4
Thailand	4.4
Malaysia	4.1
Sri Lanka	4.1
Vanuatu	4.0
Kazakhstan	3.8
Fiji	3.7
Indonesia	3.4
India	3.0
Pakistan	3.0
Lao PDR	2.7
Bangladesh	2.6
Papua New Guinea	2.5
Brunei Darussalam	2.4

High-income average 14.0%
Global average 7.1%
Developing Asia average 6.9%

% of GDP

ADB = Asian Development Bank, GDP = gross domestic product, Lao PDR = Lao People's Democratic Republic.
Source: Asian Development Bank estimates using data from the World Development Indicators, World Bank.

Projected spending estimates suggest that, between 2022 and 2026, just 17 of the world's 137 low- and middle-income economies will see government health spending increase by 1% of GDP, as recommended by the High-Level Independent Panel. The vast majority will continue to lag behind in national spending for pandemic preparedness. International support supplementing domestic efforts will need to continue until an economy has the income to finance basic healthcare. A multilateral mechanism is needed to help fund pandemic preparedness and responses in low- and middle-income economies.

A robust health system with universal health coverage can effectively support pandemic or health emergency preparedness. Osewe (2021) documents how the Republic of Korea, Thailand, and Viet Nam invested substantially in primary and preventive health infrastructure, healthcare worker recruitment and training, along with universal health coverage. These investments contributed to their successful management of the pandemic early on. The Republic of Korea was exceptional in its testing and digital contact tracing, while Viet Nam's substantial health infrastructure investment succeeded in reducing COVID-19 cases from the beginning of the pandemic. Thailand has long invested in health infrastructure—including primary health facilities, hospitals, and health worker training. Its health personnel, through regional and local health centers, successfully provided case detection, disease surveillance and community outreach in fighting the pandemic. According to the 2019 GHSI, Thailand had an overall score of 73.2 compared with the 40.2 global average; it ranked second in robust health system (70.5 compared to the 26.4 global average) and third in disease prevention (75.7 compared to the 34.8 global average). Viet Nam mandates that 30% of its budget goes toward preventive healthcare—a paradigm shift in its health system that emphasizes preventive care as a strong platform for health emergency preparedness and response. Evaluating health systems in terms of an economy's ability to provide preventive services and effective surge capacity—within the context of universal health coverage—would be useful in supporting initiatives.

With adequate healthcare financing and an insurance system, excessive out-of-pocket expenses can be avoided. Under its universal health insurance scheme, the Republic of Korea covered testing, isolation, and treatment services during the pandemic (Yoo et al. 2021).

Indonesia and Viet Nam were among countries that provided free COVID-19 isolation and treatment. Portugal granted temporary citizenship to immigrants so they could access national health services at the start of the pandemic in 2020 (Moore and Kortsaris 2020).

3.7 Policy Takeaways

Early investment that increases capacity is crucial for health systems to function efficiently and respond to emergency health needs.
Clinical institutions need to increase their capacity to screen, stabilize, and treat larger numbers of patients. They also need to shift tasks to sustain essential health services, while simultaneously increasing their ability to support regular healthcare services amidst a shortage of staff, resources, and supplies. More importantly, a "crisis standard of care" should be set to guide decision-making during health emergencies along with policies that improve healthcare worker recruitment, training, and credentialing—offering incentives as well as protection through infection control protocol and the availability of personal protective equipment (WHO 2023). Healthcare facilities need a surge plan that includes recruitment, training, and equipment supply, so the facility's service area can meet needs during a surge. Finally, health emergency simulations should be done periodically to test how surge capacity is handled.

An emergency response requires leveraging existing health capacities and platforms.
Several economies, for example, leveraged their influenza pandemic plans and capacities in developing COVID-19 response strategies. Indonesia's public health experts rapidly activated their avian influenza laboratory network to support COVID-19 efforts (Wulandari et al. 2020), while Nepal's district veterinary laboratories were converted to COVID-19 testing centers (Khanal et al. 2020). For case detection and monitoring, strong linkages are needed between testing programs, public health, and clinical institutions. In Singapore, for example, both private and university laboratories jointly conducted mass testing (WHO 2023), following 2015 agreements formed during the Middle East respiratory syndrome (MERS)–related coronavirus epidemic.

Following its experience with MERS, the Republic of Korea quickly brought private laboratories into mass testing during COVID-19 pandemic. It increased funding for disease control and prevention and strengthened system capabilities for responding to public health emergencies. It also funded a surveillance system, increased the number of professional epidemiology investigators, improved hospital infection prevention, control, and diagnostic testing. It enlisted the private sector and revised public health legislature to fast-track authorizations and enable comprehensive contact tracing.

Sustained investment and effort can help increase the number, quality, and well-being of healthcare professionals. How the healthcare workforce is made up and absorbed must be considered. An epidemiological transition requires changes in workforce skills and composition given shifting healthcare demand. More resources are needed for recruiting and training healthcare workers. Technological advances and opportunities for telemedicine and digital healthcare will affect both the skills and personnel required. This means that staffing plans will need to consider opportunities for upskilling and finding employment. During the pandemic, frontline health workers and healthcare professionals suffered mental health issues such as depression, anxiety, and insomnia (Pappa et al. 2020). Many economies experienced high levels of health worker burnout (Kaushik 2021), worsened by staff shortages and lack of workplace support in handling psychological stress. Greater attention and increased funding are needed to promote health workers' well-being and to finance burnout prevention programs. Well-defined policies on recruitment, training, and credentialing healthcare workers would help. A well-planned, flexible staffing model including training and financial incentives will be required. With many developed economies importing healthcare workers from developing economies, migration and retention policies must ensure that source economies do not face significant healthcare worker shortages (Kanchanachitra et al. 2011).

4 Data Limitations Weakened the Effectiveness of the COVID-19 Response

4.1 Data as a Basis for Policymaking

Data provide the foundation of evidence-based policymaking. Data help policymakers make well-informed decisions (Sumarto 2016). They can be used to predict the likely impact of different policy options before implementation, helping determine which policies have the highest chance of success. Data collected while monitoring implementation could serve as the basis for mid-term reviews and course corrections. Finally, data can help evaluate actual policy impact. Many stakeholders and beliefs compete for influence when forging policy. Political pressure plays a very important role (Head 2009). Data act as the crucial objective reference point during policy deliberations. Without reliable data, policies will more likely be based on ideology or political pressure (Sumarto 2016). Without data, monitoring or evaluating policies is impossible, allowing ineffective or inefficient policies to continue. For example, there is now ample evidence suggesting that school closures during COVID-19 could have ended much earlier (Shimul et al. 2024; Jakubowski, Gajderowicz, and Patrinos 2023).

The efficient use of data in policymaking is a key factor in health emergency preparedness. Robust data infrastructure was crucial to create an effective pandemic response. It enabled government agencies to conduct real-time assessments of the situation, allowing better informed decision-making (Sy et al. 2024). Kunz, Petrie, and Saxby (2024) find a relatively weak relationship between data readiness—

as defined by the 2013 Open Data Barometer—and cumulative COVID-19 mortality rates across economies 3 years into the pandemic (adjusted for population, density, age, and development status). Open Data Barometer is a global survey covering 77 economies that uses 15 indicators to measure openness and readiness of government data (Davies 2013).[4] Among ADB developing members, however, there appears to be a negative association (Figure 4.1). This suggests that better data infrastructure might have lessened the pandemic's severity. This association is indicative, as only nine ADB members are included in the Open Data Barometer.

Figure 4.1 Association between 2013 Data Readiness and Cumulative COVID-19 Mortality among ADB Developing Members

Better data infrastructure was associated with lower severity of the pandemic.

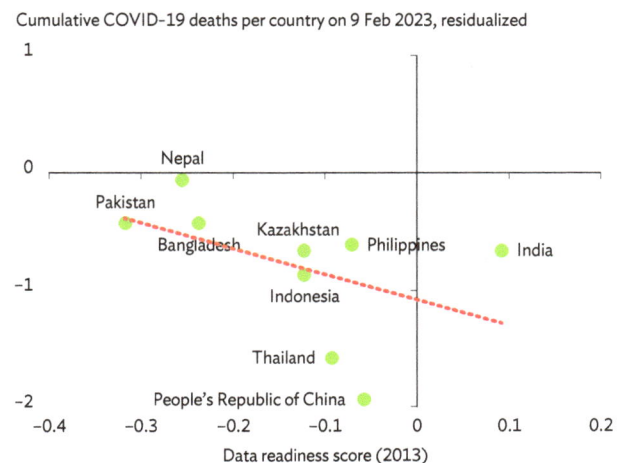

Cumulative COVID-19 deaths per country on 9 Feb 2023, residualized

Source: Kunz, Petrie, and Saxby 2024.

---

[4] There are 15 indicators: open data readiness; national data portal; open data policy; open licensing; data formats; timeliness; accessibility; accessibility for persons with disabilities; use of open data; capacity building; open data impact; open data readiness index; open data barometer score; open data quality; and open data inventory. These were created by experts, secondary data, and assessments of data availability.

4.2 Data Deficiencies among ADB Developing Members

In many economies, official health-related data are limited and outdated. Of ADB's 46 developing members, between 20 and 30 provide official data on the number of health facilities or equipment. Among these, the most recent data is from 2013 (Figure 4.2). Official subnational data are not publicly available. Ang et al. (2024a) use data collected by non-government agencies, including crowd-sourced data, to measure the number of subnational healthcare facilities. By contrast, more economies collect official census-type population registers and welfare-related data. In a recent survey, Kunz, Petrie, and Saxby (2024) reported that 32 economies had population registers, but 18 were infrequently updated. Thirty economies collect welfare-related data, with nearly half updated at least yearly.

COVID-19-related data on cases, tests, deaths, and vaccinations are widely available, but other important data are not. In some economies, data are updated daily. However, across the 46 economies, subnational data on cases and deaths are only available in 17 economies. Data on hospital bed requirements are available in only 28 economies. Just one economy provides data on daily hospital occupancy, two on ICU use, and three on weekly new hospital admissions. Disaggregated data—by sex, income group, age, and prior morbidity—are almost non-existent. It is therefore difficult to assess and understand how the pandemic affected different groups, or whether they received adequate care (Tabuga 2024).

There is also disagreement over data related to COVID-19 mortality. Actual COVID-19-related deaths appear to be more than double official reports (Figure 4.3). Cumulative excess mortality, the difference between predicted and officially reported deaths, was estimated at multiples of the official COVID-19 death figures. For example, it is estimated at 736,000 in Indonesia, around 5 times the official death figures, and 664,000 in Pakistan, around 20 times the official figures (COVID-19 Excess Mortality Collaborators 2022). Undercounting appears more prominent in low-income economies, implying it is related to limited testing capacity and low public trust in health facilities (Malik 2024).

Figure 4.2 ADB Members: Coverage and Latest Year Data Availability on Health Service Delivery

Data on health system capacity are scant and in many cases outdated.

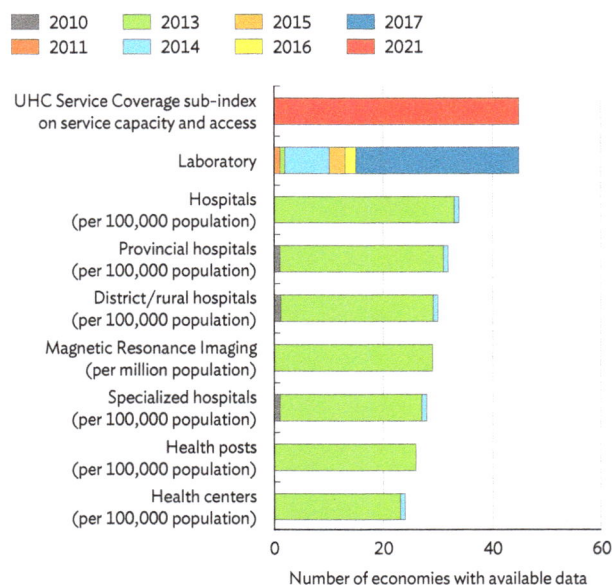

UHC = universal health coverage.
Notes: Data gathered from 45 ADB developing members, including the number of economies and latest year for each health variable. For example, data on health centers (per 100,000 population) are available in 24 economies. Of those, 2013 is the latest year for 23 economies, and 2014 for one economy.
Source: Sy et al. 2024.

Figure 4.3 Global COVID-19 Excess Mortality vs Reported Death

Cumulative excess deaths were double reported deaths.

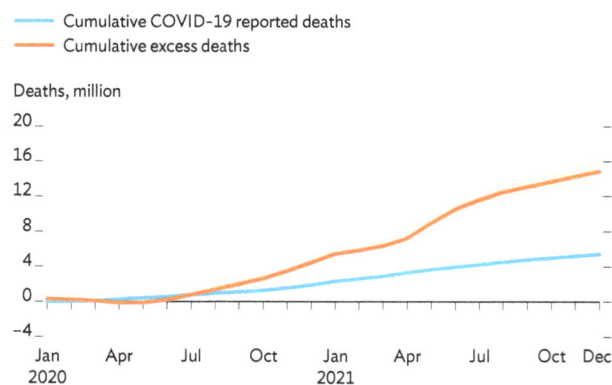

Source: Msemburi et al. 2023.

There is also evidence of data manipulation (Annaka 2021). Given the inaccuracies, understanding how policies may or may not have succeeded in controlling COVID-19 is difficult.

Administrative data are maintained but primarily used by the government agency that collected them. Overall, frequent data-sharing between agencies occurs in only about 30% of the sampled economies reported in Kunz, Petrie, and Saxby (2024). Some 10% link different administrative data (Figure 4.4). Lack of data interoperability means combining data requires entering the same data multiple times, often manually (Tabuga 2024). Finally, about 60% of member governments make administrative data available to the broader research community. This shows the largely missed opportunity to use data already collected in government business processes. Linking these data and ensuring interoperability is straightforward and would significantly increase their use in policymaking.

Figure 4.4 Selected ADB Members: Government Administrative Data Availability, Sharing, and Ability to be Linked, 2023

Governments collect many types of data, but most are not shared or linked.

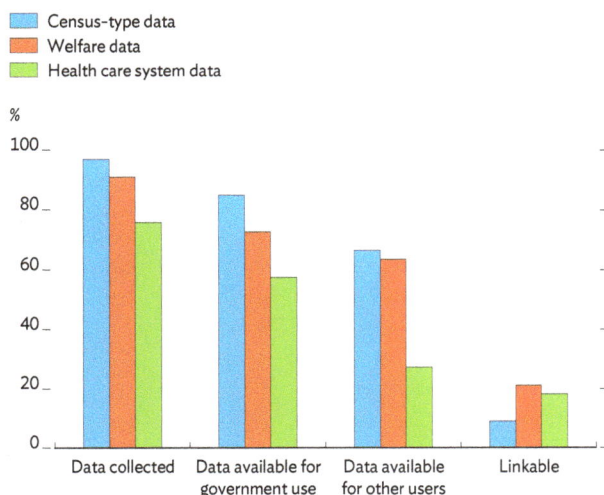

Linkable = data from other sources are interlinked.

Note: ADB members here include Armenia; Azerbaijan; Bangladesh; Bhutan; Brunei Darussalam; Cambodia; Fiji; Georgia; Hong Kong, China; India; Indonesia; Kazakhstan; the Kyrgyz Republic; the Lao People's Democratic Republic; Malaysia; Maldives; Mongolia; Nauru; Nepal; Pakistan; Papua New Guinea; the Philippines; the People's Republic of China; the Republic of the Marshall Islands; the Republic of Korea; Singapore; Solomon Islands; Sri Lanka; Taipei,China; Tajikistan; Thailand; Vanuatu; and Viet Nam.

Source: Kunz, Petrie, and Saxby 2024.

Public trust is an underlying factor. Collecting administrative data often requires the public's cooperation. Public trust in government determines people's willingness to share information and accept information provided by the government (Kunz, Petrie, and Saxby 2024). Data breaches or privacy concerns reduce confidence in sharing information. Excessive or unwelcome government surveillance, or lack of transparency and personal safety, would lead the public to withhold or provide false information. This may also result in the public having little trust in the government information provided. In turn, low trust results in low compliance with government policies. During the COVID-19 pandemic, the Republic of Korea government used individual monitoring and tracking systems, which were transparently disclosed publicly (Lee and Choi 2020). This helped compliance and cooperation.

The rapidly evolving nature of COVID-19, combined with data deficiencies, could have led researchers and policymakers to make the wrong conclusions. Data problems with COVID-19 have three dimensions. First, the frequency most government data systems were updated was incompatible with the speed at which the COVID-19 variants spread. Governments nearly always relied on data that no longer reflected the current situation. For example, modelling using the first 6 months of COVID-19 data failed to predict later outbreaks (Kuhl 2020). Second, COVID-19 surveillance methods were not standardized, with implementation quality depending on local capabilities (Struelens and Vineis 2021), and thus led to inaccuracies. Third, data quality deteriorated under pressure, hence time-series comparability was low (Stoto et al. 2022). The risk of misinterpreting data was thus high, leading to potentially wrong policy decisions. Ineffective policies reduced public trust, feeding a vicious cycle of government having to rely on increasingly inaccurate data.

4.3 Policy Takeaways

Data gathering requires sufficient infrastructure. For newly emerging diseases, rapid assessments are needed on transmissibility, infection severity, and population immunity (WHO 2023). To improve data quality and the speed it becomes available, data infrastructure must be improved.

Most important is reliable broadband internet. Kunz, Propper, and Trinh (2024) find that economies with higher broadband speed tended to have fewer COVID-19 cases (Figure 4.5). This allowed administrative and other data types to be collected faster and linked. Compared to investments in disease-specific preparedness, those for data infrastructure are more cost effective as they apply to all diseases.

Developing members should focus on harnessing administrative data. Most government administrative data between agencies currently are not linked. The trade-off between speed and accuracy (data quality) must be considered (Galaitsi et al. 2021). Investments in human capacity to use and analyze data are also needed (Kunz, Petrie, and Saxby 2024). Increasing data granularity is also important to allow analysis by different groups (Tabuga 2024).

Data sharing requires supporting regulations. Data produced outside official statistics require governments to enact regulations that ensure personal safety, privacy, data sharing, responsible use, and standardization (Ienca and Vayena 2020). More work is needed to combine government- and privately-produced data. Technology companies which collect and use big data should be offered incentives to share their data with government where there is high public interest and safety concerns. For example, keyword trends and locations in search engines could provide a mapping of public sentiment, information on resource shortages, and other frontline emergencies. International cooperation is needed so developed economies can provide financial and technical resources to developing economies to boost these capabilities.

Figure 4.5 Mobile Broadband Speed and COVID-19 Cases

Availability of faster internet is associated with lower COVID-19 cases.

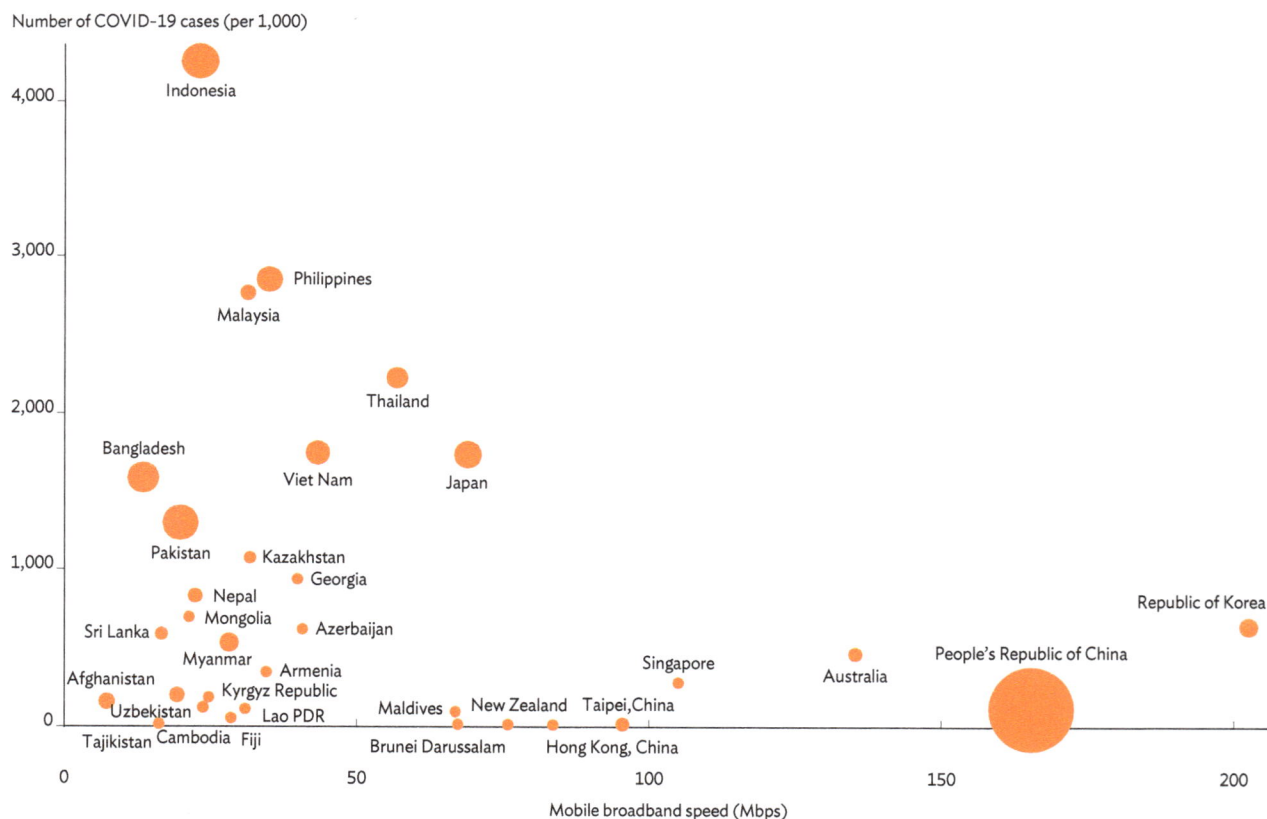

Lao PDR = Lao People's Democratic Republic.
Notes: COVID-19 data were measured as of 1 January 2023, adjusted for population. Mobile broadband speed was measured in 2020.
Source: Kunz, Propper, and Trinh 2024.

Non-traditional data sources could help narrow data gaps. During the pandemic, high-frequency data from non-traditional sources helped with data paucity. For example, the pandemic and NPI impact on economic activity were estimated using electricity market data (Fezzi and Fanghella 2020). Wastewater analysis complemented official COVID-19 test results or even replaced them in economies with weak testing (Daughton 2020). Many researchers use data from Google, both keyword searches (Kim et al. 2024b) and users' mobility to specific locations from Google Maps (Kim et al. 2024a). Finally, social media posts alerted authorities of medical supply deficiencies, and governments used mobile phone data for contact tracing and to assess the risk of contagion.

Explore the use of advanced methods combined with big data to improve predictive accuracy and evaluate policy effectiveness. Recent developments in internet broadband speed, consistency, affordability, and availability, combined with affordable smartphones allow for very large amounts of data production— so-called big data. Machine-learning algorithms, when combined with big data, offer policymakers a tool to improve the predictive accuracy of contagion. Using data for economies across the world, Sy et al. (2024) evaluate different machine-learning methods to identify proxies for health system preparedness and the responses that could best predict the extent of COVID-19 cases and mortality (Box 4.1). To evaluate policy effectiveness, Bonacini, Gallo, and Patriarca (2021) use machine learning to correctly identify the eventual impact of the first two lockdowns in Italy, just 1 day after the policies were enacted.

Box 4.1 Predicting Pandemic Outcomes with Machine-learning

More data and techniques are now available for real-time prediction of pandemic outcomes. Sy et al. (2024) collected large amounts of data for economies across the world on healthcare capacity and government responses to the COVID-19 pandemic. One challenge to real-time prediction is that some of the data is infrequent and late. The data include available information on healthcare infrastructure and services, economic activity, demographic structures, and government responses to COVID-19—both pharmaceutical and non-pharmaceutical interventions. The study pooled the data and applied machine-learning techniques to identify the optimal algorithms that work well in predicting pandemic outcomes.

Machine-learning algorithms work well in predicting outcomes when using a large dataset. Despite data limitations, the machine-learning algorithms performed well in predicting, for example, the number of COVID-19 cases and deaths with reasonable accuracy. Based on their R-square values, the methodology predicts the weekly changes in reported new cases worldwide with an 86.6% accuracy level and weekly changes in reported deaths with a 90.0% accuracy level.[a] Economies with better data availability tend to have a better prediction fit than those with more sparse data.

For example, Indonesia is a country with reasonable data availability and illustrates the model's ability to predict movements of weekly reported new cases (box figure 1).

1 Weekly Change in Reported New Cases, Indonesia

The model reasonably predicts the movements of new cases in Indonesia.

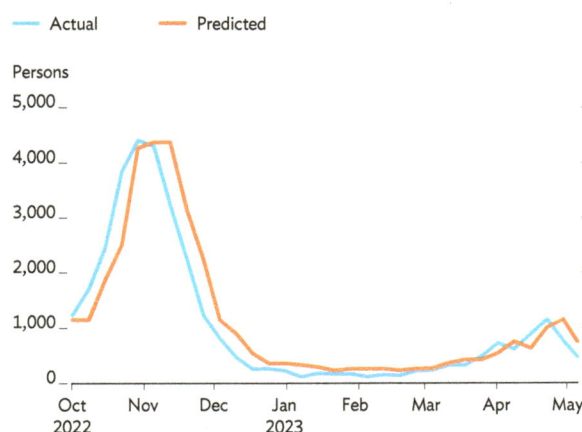

Source: S. Sy, M. Mahmud, A. Ramayandi, and D. Suryadarma. 2024. Health Infrastructure, COVID-19 Outcomes, and Factors Affecting Them. Asian Development Bank.

continued on next page

Box 4.1 *Continued*

The results can also help determine the importance of an indicator in predictions.
The Shapley values, generated using game theory to assign credit to each indicator used, showed the significance of each indicator in affecting the prediction. Sy et al. (2024) shows that demographic factors (like population size), the capacity of the healthcare system, and the comprehensiveness of government responses were key predictors for pandemic outcomes. For example, the top predictors for weekly reported deaths include a set of pre-pandemic indicators (such as population size, health system surveillance, and the more populated economies tend to see more reported deaths, while more vaccination and mobility restrictions tend to be associated with fewer deaths. Better healthcare system quality, which helped identify cases more precisely, is associated with better predictions of COVID-related deaths (box figure 2).

The models are potentially useful in upgrading health emergency preparedness. In general, the results suggest that better pre-pandemic access to quality healthcare and healthy population demographics are associated with improved overall COVID-19 outcomes. Sy et al. (2024) highlights the importance of holistic strategies in controlling the outcomes of health emergencies such as COVID-19. The findings emphasize targeted interventions, comprehensive strategies, and mobility-control measures for effective management of COVID-19 cases and deaths.

[a]   These accuracy levels are averages of sample across economies included in the exercise.

2 Weekly Changes in Reported Deaths

Top nine indicators shaping the predictions of weekly reported deaths.

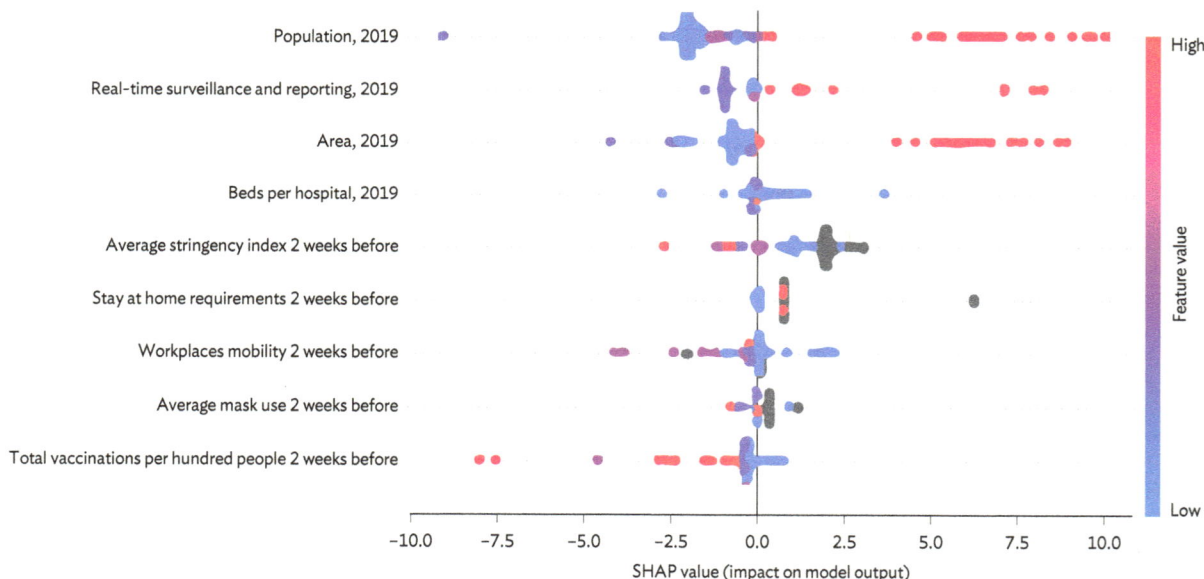

SHAP = SHapley Additive exPlanations.
Note: Higher SHAP values are related to higher prediction on reported new deaths.
Source: S. Sy, M. Mahmud, A. Ramayandi, and D. Suryadarma. 2024. Health Infrastructure, COVID-19 Outcomes, and Factors Affecting Them. Asian Development Bank.

5 What Have We Learned from the COVID-19 Response?

The COVID-19 pandemic, which swept the globe in early 2020, highlighted the critical importance of cost-effective crisis response. The pandemic's massive scale and impact left governments worldwide taking quick action without reliable guidance on the most appropriate, effective, or efficient response. In the process, it exposed the strengths and weaknesses of various response strategies. Evaluating the lessons learned will ensure greater global preparedness for future health emergencies.

Healthcare systems faced enormous challenges during the pandemic. The strain on hospitals, shortage of medical supplies, and burnout of healthcare workers all underscored the importance of evaluating and improving healthcare infrastructure. The lack of sufficient surge capacity in healthcare facilities became clear, along with diversified medical supply chains, and support systems for healthcare workers on the frontlines. Evaluating pandemic responses also exposed the disparities in public health systems. Communities with weaker healthcare infrastructure and more restricted access to quality healthcare services suffered disproportionately (Shadmi et al. 2020). There is a pressing need to evaluate and address healthcare inequalities, both within and between economies.

A critical lesson from the pandemic was the significance of data-driven decision-making. The collection and analysis of vast amounts of data drive the formation of an effective response strategy to a health crisis. It helps authorities gauge the magnitude of the crisis, formulate appropriate responses, and measure their potential and actual effectiveness. This includes data on infection rates, hospitalizations, mortality rates, vaccine distribution, and more. Governments and health organizations globally relied on data to make informed decisions on lockdowns, mask mandates, and vaccination campaigns.

The pandemic reinforced the importance of robust data collection systems, highlighting the urgent need for well-structured data infrastructure and analytical capacity. Data and information should be shared widely through appropriate communication strategies to help communicate with the public and forge trust in the authorities. Asymmetric or incomplete information led to misinformation and conspiracy theories that undermined public trust and weakened compliance with safety measures.

The pandemic response carried substantial economic and mental health costs. In addition to the disease itself, NPIs such as lockdowns and restrictions profoundly affected businesses and individuals. The need to craft economic measures such as stimulus packages and support for affected industries will help create more refined relief in the future. Mental health also emerged as a critical concern during the pandemic. Isolation, anxiety, and depression rose across society, requiring an evaluation of mental health responses and essential support systems for those affected psychologically.

The pandemic underscored the importance of preparedness for future health crises, including the need for better international cooperation. Governments and organizations must evaluate their pandemic preparedness plans and improve their capacity to deal with possible future crises—by investing in research and development for treatments, vaccines, and diagnostic tools. The pandemic demonstrated the importance of funding and continuing research to help prevent and mitigate future health emergencies. There was a scarcity of readily available finance for the procurement, logistics, and supply chains required to promptly obtain needed medical supplies, vaccines, diagnostic technologies, and medical devices. This led to the November 2022 establishment of the Pandemic Fund—a financial intermediary multi-stakeholder global partnership under World Bank auspices to better prepare for future pandemics.[5] Given the risk of global contagion, an effective response requires global collaboration. The development and distribution of vaccines, for instance, relied on multinational efforts. However, the COVID-19 pandemic also revealed shortcomings in international cooperation, with challenges in equitable vaccine distribution and vaccine nationalism. Ensuring proper mechanisms for a more equitable global response is essential.

5.1 Early Responses

The rapid spread of COVID-19 created an unprecedented global crisis and posed substantial challenges to healthcare systems across the world. As the virus quickly spread, healthcare facilities had to grapple with an overwhelming surge in patients, a dire shortage of critical medical supplies, and the mental and physical exhaustion of frontline healthcare workers. These challenges laid bare the fragility of existing healthcare infrastructure, emphasizing the urgent need for comprehensive evaluation and improvement. One of the most glaring shortcomings was the inadequacy of surge capacity. Hospitals and clinics were pushed to their limits and often hastily erected emergency facilities as authorities struggled to accommodate the influx of patients.

The early response to the pandemic was characterized by global uncertainty and rapid adjustments. Governments and health organizations around the world scrambled to understand the virus and how to contain its spread. To slow virulent contagion, many mandated measures such as strict lockdowns, travel restrictions, and social distancing. These early responses came largely from the need to buy time for healthcare systems to prepare for potential case surges and to try to learn more about the virus. However, due to the high degree of uncertainty and limited knowledge about the virus in the early days, these early responses eventually morphed into prolonged restrictions, often without publicly justifying their evolving goals and expected duration. Improving public communications when implementing NPI measures could build better trust in scientists and government, which helps determine whether people adhere to these interventions (Algan et al. 2021; Seale et al. 2020).

The pandemic brought out weaknesses in medical supply chains in many economies. The shortage of masks and other personal protective equipment, ventilators, and even basic medical supplies highlighted healthcare system vulnerability to supply chain disruptions and inadequate surge capacity. Robust healthcare infrastructure must include comprehensive stockpiling strategies to ensure adequate supply of essential medical resources during emergencies. In many economies, unorganized private initiatives often helped narrow the gap in medical supplies and complement government actions. A sufficient stockpile of medical supplies and equipment required logistic mechanisms to ensure efficient distribution.

Economies with better healthcare system quality tended to manage the pandemic better. Communities with less efficient healthcare infrastructure and limited access to services were disproportionately affected. Ahmed et al. (2024) estimate the technical efficiency score for 180 healthcare systems across the globe. They find that economies with better healthcare efficiency tended to have more vaccination coverage and lower excess mortalities during the pandemic.[6] This was confirmed by Ang et al. (2024a), who showed that economies with more efficient healthcare systems had fewer COVID-19 deaths.

Testing and contact tracing played a crucial role in early COVID-19 responses. Economies like the Republic of Korea and Taipei,China quickly implemented widespread testing and efficient technology-based contact tracing, which helped rapidly identify and isolate cases, ultimately preventing larger outbreaks. However, some economies had problems scaling up testing capacity, leading to delays in identifying and isolating those infected.

---

[5]   FAQs: The Pandemic Fund (worldbank.org).

[6]   See the discussion in section 3.

Over time, there are positive correlations between measures of available healthcare infrastructure and the number of reported COVID-19 cases across economies (Ang et al. 2024a; Sy et al. 2024). This seemingly counterintuitive observation highlights the fact that economies with stronger healthcare infrastructure tend to better detect virus spread, and hence, are better equipped to contain the worst implications of the pandemic.

Data-driven decision-making is critical in formulating responses to virus outbreaks. In the case of COVID-19, economies that swiftly gathered and analyzed data were often better prepared to respond. The ability to predict and detect outbreaks early is crucial. Data from various sources, including hospital admissions, laboratory results, and even social media, can serve as early warning signals. Sy et al. (2024) show that pre-pandemic data/information on demographic structures and health infrastructure availability and quality helped predict the number of cases across different COVID-19 variants. Higher-frequency information also improved accuracy in predicting changes in the number of COVID-19 cases and related fatalities—as data are pivotal in testing and contact tracing. Rapid and widespread testing, coupled with efficient contact tracing, helped identify and isolate cases early, which was critical in drafting strategies for controlling infectious diseases.

5.2 Cost-effectiveness of Policy Responses

The cost-effectiveness of COVID-19 responses is subject to debate. Strict lockdowns, school closures, and social distancing measures were crucial in buying time before healthcare systems became overwhelmed. But they also potentially prolonged economic downturns due to the COVID-19 response measures. These NPIs also led to immediate job losses, business closures, and reduced economic activity. School closures were among the least cost-effective policies. Governments worldwide implemented various relief and stimulus packages to mitigate the economic fallout and help ignite economic recovery. However, evidence on the relative cost-effectiveness of different measures is mixed.[7]

Every policy intervention involves trade-offs between benefits and costs. A strict lockdown, for example, could potentially have health benefits in lives saved or reduced contagion. But at the same time, it imposes economic costs that affect people's livelihoods. A prolonged strict lockdown would in turn create other health issues, like depression and untreated non-COVID illnesses, which reduce the lockdown's health benefits.

Gauging the cost-effectiveness of COVID-19 responses will help devise strategies in preparing for a future pandemic. Cost-effectiveness analysis assesses the efficiency of different interventions or strategies in terms of their costs and the health outcomes they produce. Shimul et al. (2024) evaluate the costs of common interventions—including mask-wearing, school closures, social distancing, and vaccinations—in terms of their dollar costs per Disability-Adjusted Life Years (DALY) averted for selected economies with varying characteristics. The study suggests that not all interventions are equally cost-effective across economies, implying that country context must be considered when devising any intervention policy.

In general, pharmaceutical interventions were more cost-effective than NPIs. To estimate the cost-effectiveness of policy interventions, Shimul et al. (2024) simulate the dollar value of the cost per DALY averted for a sample of different policy interventions during the pandemic in five countries with available data and calibrated SEIRS model.[8]

---

[7] These pieces of evidence were almost non-existent ex-ante, when both the costs and effectiveness of these measures were unknown. It was also unclear whether the cost-effectiveness of COVID-19 NPIs would necessarily translate to a novel pandemic with different transmission patterns and/or age structure burden. For example, school closures might be a very important measure for a pandemic where children are particularly vulnerable.

[8] SEIRS is an acronym for susceptible-exposed-infectious-recovered-susceptible. The model was created by the COVID-19 International Modelling Consortium (CoMo Consortium—www.comomodel.net). It allows an estimation of the trajectory of COVID-19 based on scenarios and assessments of the impact of different NPIs and pharmaceutical interventions.

Interventions are considered cost-effective when their cost per DALY averted is less than a country's GDP per capita (Robinson et al. 2017). Vaccinations were highly cost-effective across economies (Table 5.1). By contrast, school closures appeared less cost-effective and highly cost-ineffective in several economies. The potential long-term costs of lost learning, labor productivity, and human capital due to school closures were much higher than the DALY averted. Although school closures were substantial even in a high-income economy like the Republic of Korea, their costs tend to be higher where access to the internet and digital devices is limited—learning losses from school closures would be worse (Maddawin et al. 2024).

The cost implications of policy interventions vary across economies. The cost-effectiveness of the same type of intervention may not be the same in all economies, as specific factors affecting the economy greatly influence the number of lives saved. For example, mask-wearing is relatively less cost-effective for lower-income economies due to the high costs of mask distribution. Mobility restrictions tend to be more cost-effective in economies with high population density than those with low density. Most interventions—including free mask distribution—were relatively cost-effective for high-income economies.

Mixing policy interventions was more cost-effective than applying policies individually. The need for school closures, for example, could be avoided if other stronger NPIs were adopted appropriately. The costs per DALY averted can also be measured by considering a suite of interventions when dealing with the virus. To do so, it must be clear which policy combinations are included in the intervention mix. The intervention package taken by the Republic of Korea is often considered ideal.[9] However, if applied to Bangladesh during the first year of the pandemic, for example, it would have been just as cost-effective as the actual policy mix Bangladesh used (Shimul et al. 2024). Thus, Bangladesh would not have gained if it had adopted the Republic of Korea's package. Also, Bangladesh could not afford the financial costs of implementing the package. In short, the capacity to deploy response packages is also constrained by an economy's income level. Governments should consider affordability in deciding the intervention mix.

Table 5.1 Cost-effectiveness of Vaccines and Non-Pharmaceutical Interventions during the COVID-19 Pandemic

Vaccinations outperformed non-pharmaceutical measures in cost-effectiveness.

	Vaccinations	Mask Wearing	School Closures	Mobility Restrictions	
				Strict	Partial
Bangladesh	0.52	8.61	6.23	1.37	0.10
Georgia	0.09	0.47	0.63	10.86	17.24
Republic of Korea	0.37	3.61	43.32	0.37	0.41
Thailand	0.14	0.10	0.10	1.77	0.06
Uzbekistan	0.02	0.48	3.49	0.71	1.24

Source: Calculated from Shimul et al. 2024.

---

9   The package took strong tracing, testing, and treatment measures. It digitalized the epidemiological investigation process, mandated strict quarantines for inbound travelers, made diagnostic tests widely available, developed test kits, and established national security safe hospitals and life treatment centers.

5.3 Lessons Learned from COVID-19 Response

5.3.1 Type of Interventions and Relief Efforts

Response programs were designed and implemented to effectively manage the harm done by the pandemic. For example, ADB COVID-19 support included finance, knowledge, and partnerships to mitigate the social and economic effects of the pandemic on people and business. Support to developing member became a set of interrelated programs and interventions that addressed direct and indirect pandemic effects. These included various health-related programs, social relief efforts, social assistance to the poor and vulnerable people, and various types of support for affected businesses and workers.

Health-related responses typically focused on providing effective quarantine facilities, testing capacity, and COVID-19 treatment. Ventilators, protective kits, and other equipment to prevent infection were procured to treat the affected population. Critical care beds for COVID-19 treatment and isolation beds were made available in health facilities. For a specified period, treatment was publicly funded, with no out-of-pocket expenses for patients. Support for medical workers came via cash incentives along with mental health and safety protocols. Training to prepare and equip health workers and volunteers was conducted to narrow gaps in capacity. Volunteers were also mobilized for rapid response and contact tracing, while online COVID-19 database management or surveillance systems were set up to manage these rapid responses and interrelated work. Health sector budgets were also monitored to ensure normal health programs could continue.

Relief efforts and social assistance provided basic necessities, income support and childcare, and incentives for healthcare personnel.
As mobility restrictions limited the ability to meet basic needs, relief efforts supplied food and other necessities such as utilities and basic medical supplies. Cash transfers were prioritized to maintain the purchasing power of the poor and vulnerable.

A crucial lesson from these relief operations was the importance of rationing enough food to last over an extended period, as logistics made frequent relief operations difficult. Other assistance included childcare support and benefits.

Expanding the coverage of existing social assistance programs helped expedite relief efforts. Established emergency systems for identifying and distributing the relief needed helped expedite implementing interventions. Expanding coverage of existing social assistance or poverty identification programs—such as the Family Hope Program in Indonesia, the Targeted Social Assistance Program in Tajikistan, the IDPoor program in Cambodia, the National Old Age Program in Bangladesh, and the Kifalat Program in Pakistan—benefited more people and proved useful in quickly identifying target recipients of relief efforts and social assistance programs.

Financing support for businesses and workers helped those heavily affected by the pandemic. Lockdowns and mobility restrictions also created significant business and job losses. Business and worker support included financing, tax-related programs, support for wages and payrolls, and job support. These helped companies and businesses maintain operational capacity and protect worker livelihoods. Subsidized loans helped ensure business continuity, adequate supplies, and distribution. Loan extensions and restructuring were also offered to small and medium-sized enterprises (SMEs) and agricultural entrepreneurs. Temporary tax holidays and tax incentives were given to both industries and workers. Temporary tax relief or deductions were also provided to SMEs operating mainly in manufacturing, tourism, garments, textiles, and footwear.

Income support helped maintain workers' purchasing power. Wage subsidies, cash handouts, and payroll support were extended to affected workers to protect their livelihoods. Unemployment benefits were also given to workers whose jobs were lost due to the pandemic. Other types of livelihood and productivity support were also used, such as employment subsidies via cash-for-work programs targeting women, disadvantaged groups, and the unemployed. Assistance was also given to migrant workers by way of temporary accommodation and repatriation support.

5.3.2 Issues and Lessons

The multiple facets of COVID-19 responses offer lessons for the future. Lessons drawn from the pandemic revolve around key themes that emphasize the importance of needs-based approaches. These are shown, for example, in a content analysis of completion reports of ADB projects supporting programs on COVID-19 responses (Figure 5.1). Other significant themes involve time, data, effective measures and implementation, financial resources, health impact, social assistance, effective targeting, and gender.

Quick relief and preventive measures are basic to a health emergency response. Providing relief—such as food, basic commodities, and health services—to the most vulnerable population is paramount, along with preventive measures such as providing quarantine and testing facilities, personal protective equipment, and ensuring minimal disruption to food supply and other basic goods and services. These all require timely fund disbursement and deployment of human resources—allowing essential service personnel to work safely.

Technical assistance grants—such as supplying personal protective equipment and diagnostic kits—significantly helped fight the pandemic. Examples from Timor-Leste, the Kyrgyz Republic, Sri Lanka, India, and Bhutan underscored the importance of prompt implementation during critical periods. In Bhutan, the immediate response and active surveillance supported effective planning and decision making. Adequate preparation through established systems—like India's social protection frameworks and the Cook Islands' digital payment systems—played a key role in mobilizing social safety nets.

Close coordination with local and national governments and other relief teams can ease the pressures of limited food and other supplies. Distributing relief items and medical equipment can be made more efficient through context-specific logistic strategies. For instance, in the Pacific, using a hub (like Fiji) to cover several island economies made distributing medical supplies more efficient than going directly to each economy.

Figure 5.1 Word Cloud related to Issues and Lessons

Needs-based programs, led by government and supported by development partners, are crucial for health emergency responses.

Source: Tabuga 2024.

Any challenges, logistical or otherwise, can be fixed by properly assessing a recipient community's physical environment. Coordinating with local authorities and non-government partners is essential.

Strengthening preparedness is key. Urgent decision making and early program implementation during the pandemic's initial stage led to some aspects being overlooked during planning. The importance of preparation, therefore, cannot be overemphasized. Systems already in place prior to the pandemic allowed for quick mobilization during the crisis. These include existing legal frameworks that enable proper budgeting and timely disbursement of funds, social protection frameworks, and effective systems for public distribution and benefit transfers. There were also established digital payment systems including tax evaluation and superannuation systems, investments in emergency operation centers and laboratories that can handle new viruses. Conducting regular simulations was extremely useful. Existing national registers for the poor and vulnerable were instrumental in the speedy distribution of cash transfers and other benefits. Establishing these registers or enhancing their coverage to include all vulnerable groups and strengthening data systems and their interoperability during normal times is essential.

Crisis response must be mainstreamed into the broader macroeconomic agenda. Existing policies must be more proactive—to allow flexibility in accommodating emerging issues and make entire systems respond more rapidly. Stronger political will is required to establish or strengthen information systems—with data granularity and interoperability—for surveillance, monitoring, and targeting. Development agencies like ADB should establish a financing modality dedicated for health crises and other emergencies. ADB's countercyclical support facility—the COVID-19 Pandemic Response Option—was lauded for its success in addressing the emergency needs during a health crisis.

Flexibility emerged as a critical factor in preparing for future health emergencies. Targeting, monitoring, and capacity-building must be adaptable, considering factors beyond the control of implementing teams. During crises, a flexible approach to program target-setting can more easily adapt to changing needs.

For example, online training can replace face-to-face sessions, and assistance should be adjusted based on government capacity. Anticipating some program disruptions and being prepared to innovate is essential. Innovations in coordination and team structure played a pivotal role in ensuring the timely delivery of support during the pandemic. It highlighted the importance of effective communication strategies, transparent reporting on fund utilization, and the need for future emergency relief plans to account for nuanced contextual factors and constraints.

Data, monitoring and evaluation systems must be strengthened. Governments and development partners must prioritize data system development and enhancement to allow for effective communication strategies in managing responses. It is important that economies and their partners develop or update national registries to improve targeting and interoperability. Better screening processes for support programs will limit program leakage and facilitate the smooth disbursement of benefits. In addition, there must be continuous monitoring, frequent reporting, integrated information systems at various government levels (local, provincial, federal), and effective knowledge management.

Strategic partnerships with private entities also made important contributions to the pandemic response. The private sector became both a partner and recipient of assistance. Leveraging capacities in laboratory development and manufacturing medical countermeasures contributed to successful COVID-19 testing and supply of personal protective equipment. Partnering with the private sector, however, requires careful attention to not-for-profit public–private partnerships, tax regulations, and logistics coordination. Governments also collaborated with the private sector and civil society organizations on vaccination programs, which emphasized the benefits of strategic partnerships in responding to crises.

5.3.3 Coordination and Partnerships

Coordination and partnerships were vital in delivering COVID-19 responses. Collaboration and teamwork across the processes of program design, implementation, monitoring and targeting, and financing allowed for a smooth delivery of COVID-19 responses. There were nuances in coordination structure, including the various entities involved, that played important roles in pandemic response efforts. Developing response strategies and financial plans benefited greatly from policy dialogue and stakeholder consultations—including development partners and government agencies along with civil society and private sector partners.

Strong collaboration and coordination helped overcome the many challenges. Participatory approaches that promote regular contact and communication can resolve the challenges and pressures emanating from uncertain, constantly evolving health and economic situations. They helped devise simultaneous and dynamic guidelines for intervention policies. Close collaboration among development partners resulted in successful co-financing of programs as well as in providing technical expertise for their implementation. Its close alignment and continuous policy dialogue with governments contributed to effective program implementation. Likewise, government partnerships with community-based organizations also helped target and reach beneficiaries, along with understanding challenges on the ground and to get feedback as response efforts were being implemented. In program monitoring, close coordination and shared reporting reduced the burden from numerous reporting requirements and competing demands for staff time.

Successful implementation of pandemic response programs was attributed to broad partnerships, close coordination, flexibility, and risk-taking. Continuous dialogue and participatory approaches between governments and their development partners helped program design, led to co-financing, and addressed implementation challenges. Expert advice aided program design and monitoring, with technical advisers providing economic analyses and impact assessments. The flexibility demonstrated in program design, implementation approaches, and budget allocation was crucial in responding effectively to the urgent and evolving pandemic needs. This adaptability allowed for the reallocation of funds, innovative approaches, and adjustments required in response to the crisis.

Coordination and partnerships helped build resilience to health emergencies. When dealing with a time-sensitive health emergency with many uncertainties, it is essential to exchange ideas and experience in installing flexibility in policy formulation and implementation. Unprecedented crises like the COVID-19 pandemic call for coordinated responses nationally, regionally, and globally. There are incentives for all economies, rich and poor, to coordinate and invest in future collaborative frameworks to intervene against health emergencies, be it pharmaceutical or non-pharmaceutical interventions. Continuous investments in building a scientific knowledge base and capitalizing on the lessons from the pandemic can build better resilience against future emergencies.

5.4 Policy Takeaways

Investments in healthcare infrastructure and preparedness must be prioritized. Policymakers need to comprehensively evaluate and improve healthcare infrastructure, including greater surge capacity. The COVID-19 pandemic exposed the vulnerability of healthcare systems to disruptions in supply chains, emphasizing the need for robust stockpiling strategies for essential medical resources. Effective emergency response requires ensuring stockpiles are sufficient, coupled with efficient logistic mechanisms for distribution. It is also important to be cautious and avoid overinvesting in pandemic-specific preparedness, as predicting pandemics is virtually impossible. Thus, investing in general preparedness will likely be more cost effective.

Healthcare system efficiency and quality should be enhanced. Economies with more efficient healthcare systems better managed the pandemic and had higher vaccination rates and fewer excess mortalities. Policymakers should focus on improving the technical efficiency of healthcare systems, ensuring better access to healthcare services, and addressing disparities. This involves strategic planning, resource allocation, and continuous evaluation of healthcare system performance.

Data-driven decision-making and early response strategies should be prioritized. Policymakers should prioritize data-driven decision-making in formulating responses to virus outbreaks. Swift data gathering and analysis enable better preparation and response. Pre-pandemic data, including demographic structures and health infrastructure quality was important in predicting and managing the spread of COVID-19. Policymakers should invest in data infrastructure, leverage diverse data sources, and emphasize the importance of early warning signals for effective testing, contact tracing, and overall infectious disease control. Lessons from the pandemic response underscore the significance of quick decision-making and rapid program implementation, ensuring timely disbursement of funds and deployment of resources. Nonetheless, even when data are available, decisions must be made with a high degree of uncertainty.

Interventions work best when tailored to an economy's specific context. Policymakers should recognize that the cost-effectiveness of COVID-19 interventions varied across economies. The cost-effectiveness of the same measure differs by economy. Socioeconomic context, such as population density, demographic characteristics, income levels, and infrastructure readiness must be considered in devising intervention policies. When exposed to health emergencies, pharmaceutical interventions should be prioritized whenever possible, as they are more cost effective than NPIs. Policymakers should allocate resources efficiently, considering the long-term intervention costs. A policy mix based on an economy's specific needs and challenges will be more effective than individual measures.

Mainstream crisis response into macroeconomic policies. Crisis response must be integrated into the broader macroeconomic agenda, emphasizing proactive policies and flexible systems that can accommodate emerging issues. Strengthening coordination among entities involved makes resource use more efficient. Building local capacities for future emergencies is a priority. At the same time, ensuring a sustainable long-term recovery involves addressing key areas such as the business and investment climate, resilient social protection systems, sound public finance management, and sustainable agriculture for food security. Maintaining a strong macroeconomic foundation can speed up crisis recovery. This involves building cash and fiscal buffers while maintaining low and stable public debt levels. International financing also helps governments ensure sufficient liquidity in the domestic private sector during crises.

Build on the flexibility, innovation, and collaboration needed for future health emergencies. A flexible approach to program target-setting, online training, and innovative coordination strategies is essential. It should include effective communications, transparent reporting on fund utilization, and future emergency relief plans that consider each economy's strengths and weaknesses. Strengthening data, monitoring, and evaluation systems is needed for continuous monitoring, frequent reporting, and knowledge management. Strategic partnerships with private entities, including careful consideration of public–private partnerships, tax regulations, and logistics coordination, are essential elements in crafting a crisis response. Learning from the COVID-19 experience, continuous investments in scientific knowledge and collaboration frameworks can help build resilience against future pandemics.

Background Papers for this Report

Ahmed, S., M. Mahmud, A. Ramayandi, and D. Suryadarma. 2024. Health Systems Efficiency and its Association with COVID-19 Outcomes in Selected Economies. Asian Development Bank.

The paper examines the association between health system efficiency and COVID-19 health outcomes. Using data envelopment analysis, the technical efficiency of health systems in 189 economies are estimated with both pre- and post-COVID-19 health outcomes. The paper finds that health systems with higher technical efficiency experienced more favorable COVID-19 outcomes.

Ang, R., M. Mahmud, A. Ramayandi, and D. Suryadarma. 2024a. Access to Healthcare Facilities and COVID-19 Outcomes: Evidence from Selected Asian Economies. Asian Development Bank.

The paper estimates the correlation between healthcare facilities (by number, travel time to the closest, and concentration) and COVID-19 outcomes (in cases, mortality, and vaccinations). Using subnational data from 11 ADB members, it finds that having more healthcare facilities should better detect cases and deaths, and increase vaccination rates.

———. 2024b. COVID-19 Preparedness, Responses, and Outcomes: A Cross-country Analysis. Asian Development Bank.

The paper examines the correlation between a country's health security, health system efficiency, and prior experience with respiratory pathogen pandemics to COVID-19 cases, mortality, and vaccination rates. The evidence suggests that prior experience with a respiratory pathogen like SARS is associated with lower COVID-19 cases.

Armstrong-Mensah, E. 2024. Planning For Future Global Health Emergencies in Asia and the Pacific Post COVID-19: Strategies and Investments for Risk Prevention, Preparedness, Detection, and Response. Asian Development Bank.

The paper summarizes country responses to previous respiratory pathogen pandemics, such as SARS and MERS. It also examines whether countries learned from their experience and strengthened their public health systems. The paper uses various global secondary data and a literature review to provide key takeaways related to building health emergency preparedness.

Bhatia, R. 2024. India's Health Sector Response to COVID-19 Pandemic. Asian Development Bank.

The COVID-19 pandemic caused significant social, economic, and health consequences. It strained healthcare systems, with hospitals and medical professionals facing overwhelming challenges in managing the influx of patients in both developing and developed economies. India was one of the most affected countries. Its health system was overwhelmed and its response made it an interesting case study. Several critical lessons stood out on how to strengthen its health system to mitigate the impact of future public health emergencies.

Kim, S., K. Koh, and M. Mahmud. 2024a. The COVID-19 Pandemic and Psychological Well-being in Asian Economies. Asian Development Bank.

The paper examines the relationship between government-imposed non-pharmaceutical interventions (NPIs) during the COVID-19 pandemic and people's psychological well-being (PWB) using Google's high-frequency cross-country search index data on depressive symptoms. It finds significant cross-country heterogeneity in PWB patterns and shows that higher government stringency in implementing NPIs due to pandemic severity worsened PWB. Overall, the study contributes to the literature on PWB impacts of the COVID-19 pandemic, particularly in Asia, and provides valuable insights for policymakers and researchers in understanding the effects of government responses on mental health during a global health emergency.

Kim, S., K. Koh, and A. Ramayandi. 2024b.
Government Responses to the COVID-19
Pandemic and Their Economic Consequences.
Asian Development Bank.

*The paper examines the relationships between
government non-pharmaceutical interventions
(NPIs) and macroeconomic outcomes (such as
GDP and unemployment) during the COVID-19
pandemic using country-level panel data from
165 economies. Those using stricter NPIs (school
closures, workplace closures, and international travel
bans) saw larger reductions in GDP per capita.
However, stricter NPIs did not appear to accelerate
economic recovery the following year. This suggests
they were accompanied by deteriorating economic
growth, with the negative relationships lasting longer
than expected. The dynamic and heterogeneity
analysis results also indicate that the impacts
could differ by NPI intensity and across economies.
This suggests designing optimal NPI policies for
future pandemics will be quite complex.*

Kunz, J., D. Petrie, and K. Saxby. 2024. Data
Preparedness for Continuous Policy Evaluation in
Health Emergencies. Asian Development Bank.

*The paper discusses how administrative data
can be used to provide evidence to better inform
policy responses during health emergencies.
Data availability, frequency of collection, and
linkages between sources help determine data
preparedness across ADB DMCs. It also discusses
the trade-offs between monitoring and evaluation
and provides recommendations to governments on
how best to maximize the use of administrative data
to effectively target policy responses.*

Kunz, J., C. Propper, and T. Trinh. 2024. The Impact
of Internet Access on COVID-19 Spread in
Indonesia. Asian Development Bank.

*The COVID-19 pandemic highlighted the crucial
role internet access played in pandemic prevention
and response. Internet access facilitated the rapid
dissemination of vital information, provided
telemedicine services, and enabled remote work
and education. The study uses a wide range of data
sources to investigate the geographic variation of
internet access proxied by 3G mobile broadband
during the pandemic in Indonesia. It uses several
approaches to account for possible confounding
factors, including lightning strikes as an instrumental
variable, to confirm the significant role the
internet played in the spread of COVID-19 cases.
The findings suggest that increasing internet access
could help pandemic prevention and response,
particularly in regions with limited connectivity.
Therefore, improving internet infrastructure in
developing economies may be crucial in preventing
future pandemics.*

Malik, M. 2024. Exploring Bias in Measurement of
COVID-19 Impact: How Significant was the
Undercounting? Asian Development Bank.

*National authorities' official statistics do not paint
a comprehensive picture of the COVID-19 impact.
Particularly in Sub-Saharan Africa and South Asia,
the actual impact appeared to be much higher.
This highlights the need to strengthen disease
surveillance and remove political barriers to accurate
reporting. To close data gaps, national health
information systems need to report causes of death
and integrate surveillance across regions.*

Shimul, S., M. Mahmud, A. Ramayandi, and
D. Suryadarma. 2024. Simulating Cost
Effectiveness of COVID-19 Policy
Responses: Cases of Five Asian Countries.
Asian Development Bank.

*For selected Asian economies, this paper investigates
the trade-offs between different COVID-19
interventions and their cost-effectiveness in
terms of cost per disability-adjusted life years
averted. Cost effectiveness is compared across
six interventions, including mask-wearing, school
closures, social distancing, and vaccinations.
It finds vaccinations were most cost-effective in all
sample economies, with the cost-effectiveness of
other interventions varying by economy.*

Sy, S., M. Mahmud, A. Ramayandi, and D. Suryadarma. 2024. Health Infrastructure, COVID-19 Outcomes, and Factors Affecting Them. Asian Development Bank.

The study provides an overview of the COVID-19 pandemic's impact in Asia; its outcomes, healthcare capacity, and government responses. The effects varied across economies due to disparities in health capacity and government response. The research builds a machine-learning model that predicts COVID-19 outcomes based on a comprehensive set of features, including government response and country demographics worldwide. After evaluating alternative machine learning algorithms, Gradient Boosting Regression, LightGBM, and XGBoost perform best in predicting new weekly cases, deaths, and excess mortality, respectively. These global trend predictions should help lead to more informed governmental responses. Higher population and available facilities are correlated with increased reported cases, while more vaccinations and mask usage are linked to reduced cases. Population and the comprehensiveness of government responses were key predictors of reported cases, highlighting the importance of holistic strategies. Conversely, for reported deaths and excess mortality, top predictors were population, vaccinations, and containment policies/mobility. Thus, targeted interventions, comprehensive strategies, and mobility control better manage COVID-19 cases and deaths.

Tabuga, A. 2024. Development Cooperation in the Management of Global Health Emergency: A Synthesis of Lessons Learned from the Asian Development Bank's COVID-19 Response. Asian Development Bank.

As of November 2021, ADB's financing assistance to 41 developing members reached $24.6 billion. Apart from financing, ADB provides knowledge and partnerships to its developing members. The paper summarizes the lessons from relevant ADB project completion reports.

References

Abiad, A., C. R. Jabagat, E. Laviña, J. Pagaduan, and R. Platitas. 2020. The Impact of COVID-19 on Developing Asia: The Pandemic Extends into 2021. *Asian Development Bank Briefs*, No. 159.

ADB. 2022. Pandemic Sets Back Fight Against Poverty in Asia by At Least 2 Years, Has Likely Hurt Social Mobility.

Aksunger, N., C. Vernot, R. Littman, M. Voors, N. F. Meriggi, A. Abajobir, et al. 2023. COVID-19 and Mental Health in 8 Low- and Middle-income Countries: A Prospective Cohort Study. *PLoS Med* 20(4): e1004081.

Algan, Y., D. Cohen, E. Davoine, and S. Stantcheva. 2021. Trust in Scientists in Times of Pandemic: Panel Evidence from 12 Countries. *Proceedings of the National Academy of Sciences* 118(40). e2108576118.

Alizadeh, H., A. Sharifi, S. Damanbagh, et al. 2023. Impacts of the COVID-19 Pandemic on the Social Sphere and Lessons for Crisis Management: A Literature Review. *Natural Hazards* 117, 2139–2164.

Annaka, S. 2021. Political Regime, Data Transparency, and COVID-19 Death Cases. *SSM – Population Health* 15, 100832.

Ashraf, B. N. and J. Goodell. 2022. COVID-19 Social Distancing Measures and Economic Growth: Distinguishing Short- and Long-term Effects. *Finance Research Letters* 47. Part A.

Bell, J. and J. B. Nuzzo. 2021. Global Health Security Index: Advancing Collective Action and Accountability Amid Global Crisis. www.GHSIndex.org.

Bonacini, L., G. Gallo, and F. Patriarca. 2021. Identifying Policy Challenges of COVID-19 in Hardly Reliable Data and Judging the Success of Lockdown Measures. *Journal of Population Economics* 34. 275–301.

Brodeur, A., A. Clark, S. Fleche, and N. Powdthavee. 2021. COVID-19, Lockdowns and Well-Being: Evidence from Google Trends. *Journal of Public Economics* 193.

Chetty, R., J. N. Friedman, N. Hendren, and M. Stepner. 2020. The Economic Impacts of COVID-19: Evidence from a New Public Database Built Using Private Sector Data. National Bureau of Economic Research (27431).

Cohen, S., S. Chakravarthy, S. Bharathi, B. Narayanan, and C. Park. 2022. Potential Economic Impact of COVID-19-Related School Closures. *ADB Economic Working Paper Series*, No. 657. Asian Development Bank.

COVID-19 Excess Mortality Collaborators. 2022. Estimating Excess Mortality Due to the COVID-19 Pandemic: A Systematic Analysis of COVID-19-Related Mortality, 2020–21. *The Lancet* 399(10334). 1513–1536.

Daughton, C. G. 2020. Wastewater Surveillance for Population-wide COVID-19: The Present and Future. *Science of the Total Environment* 736. 139631.

Davies, T. 2013. Open Data Barometer: 2013 Global Report. World Wide Web Foundation and Open Data Institute.

Deb, P., D. Furceri, J. D. Ostry, and N. Tawk. 2022. The Economic Effects of COVID-19 Containment Measures. *Open Econ Rev* 33(1). 1–32.

Dela Cruz, N. A., A. J. Adona, R. Molato-Gayares, and A. Park. 2024. Learning Loss and Recovery from the COVID-19 Pandemic: A Systematic Review of Evidence. *ADB Economics Working Paper Series* No. 717. Asian Development Bank.

Emmerling, J., D. Furceri, F. L. Monteiro, P. Loungani, J. Ostry, P. Pizzuto, and M. Tavoni. 2021. Will the Economic Impact of COVID-19 Persist? Prognosis from 21st Century Pandemics. *IMF Working Paper* 21/119. International Monetary Fund.

European Centre for Disease Prevention and Control. 2023. Lessons from the COVID-19 Pandemic. Stockholm: ECDC.

Excler, J. L., M. Saville, L. Privor-Dumm, S. Gilbert, P. J. Hotez, D. Thompson, S. Abdool-Karim, and J. H. Kim. 2023. Factors, Enablers and Challenges for COVID-19 Vaccine Development. *BMJ Global Health* 8(6).

Fezzi, C. and V. Fanghella. 2020. Real-Time Estimation of the Short-Run Impact of COVID-19 on Economic Activity using Electricity Market Data. *Environmental & Resource Economics* 76. 885–900.

Flaxman, S., S. Mishra, A. Gandy, et al. 2020. Estimating the Effects of Non-pharmaceutical Interventions on COVID-19 in Europe. *Nature* 584. 257–261.

Galaitsi, S. E., J. C. Cegan, K. Volk, M. Joyner, B. D. Trump, and I. Linkov. 2021. The Challenges of Data Usage for the United States' COVID-19 Response. *International Journal of Information Management* 59. 102352.

Gentilini, U. 2022. Cash Transfers in Pandemic Times: Evidence, Practices, and Implications from the Largest Scale up in History. World Bank.

Global Burden of Disease 2021 Health Financing Collaborator Network. 2023. Global Investments in Pandemic Preparedness and COVID-19: Development Assistance and Domestic Spending on Health Between 1990 and 2026. *Lancet Global Health* 11. e385-413.

Hale, T., N. Angrist, R. Goldszmidt, et al. 2021. A Global Panel Database of Pandemic Policies (Oxford COVID-19 Government Response Tracker). *Nature Human Behavior* 5. 529–538.

Head, B. 2009. Evidence-based Policy: Principles and Requirements, in Productivity Commission. *Strengthening Evidence-based Policy in the Australian Federation. Volume 1: Proceedings.* Roundtable Proceedings. Productivity Commission Canberra.

Ienca, M. and E. Vayena. 2020. On the Responsible Use of Digital Data to Tackle the COVID-19 Pandemic. *Nature Medicine* 26. 463–464.

International Health Regulations (IHR). 2005. https://www.who.int/publications/i/item/9789241580496. World Health Organization.

Jakubowski, M., T. Gajderowicz, and H. A. Patrinos. 2023. Global Learning Loss in Student Achievement: First Estimates Using Comparable Reading Scores. *Economics Letters* 232.

Joaquim, R., A. Pinto, R. Guatimosim, J. de Paula, D. Souza Costa, A. P. Diaz, A. da Silva, M. Pinheiro, A. Serpa, D. Miranda, and L. Malloy-Diniz. 2021. Bereavement and Psychological Distress During COVID-19 Pandemics: The Impact of Death Experience on Mental Health. *Current Research in Behavioral Sciences* 2.

Kanchanachitra, C., M. Lindelow, T. Johnston, P. Hanvoravongchai, F. M. Lorenzo, N. L. Huong, S. A. Wilopo, and J. F. dela Rosa. 2011. Human Resources for Health in Southeast Asia: Shortages, Distributional Challenges, and International Trade in Health Services. *The Lancet* 377(9767). 769–781.

Kaushik, D. 2021. COVID-19 and Health Care Workers Burnout: A Call for Global Action. *The Lancet* 35. 100808.

Khanal, A., A. Gautam, D. Subedi, S. Bhandari, and K. Kaphle. 2020. Contribution of Veterinary Sector to Control COVID-19 Pandemic in Nepal. *World Veterinary Journal* 10(3). 297–305.

Kodama, W., T. Long, D. Azhgaliyeva, P. Morgan, and K. Kim. 2023. Family Business during the COVID-19 Pandemic in Asia: Role of Government Financial Aid and Coping Strategies. *ADBI Working Paper* 1405. Asian Development Bank Institute.

König, M. and A. Winkler. 2021. The Impact of Government Responses to the COVID-19 Pandemic on GDP Growth: Does Strategy Matter? *PLOS ONE* 16(11).

Kremer, M. 2023. The Economics of Investing in COVID-19 Vaccines: Implications for the Asian Development Bank. *Asian Development Review* 40(1). 1–12.

Kubota, S., K. Onishi, and Y. Toyama. 2021. Consumption Responses to COVID-19 Payments: Evidence from a Natural Experiment and Bank Account Data. *Journal of Economic Behavior & Organization* 188. 1–17.

Kuhl, E. 2020. Data-driven Modeling of COVID-19-Lessons Learned. *Extreme Mechanics Letters* 40. 100921.

Lee, D. and B. Choi. 2020. Policies and Innovations to Battle COVID-19 – A Case Study of South Korea. *Health Policy and Technology* 9(4). 587–597.

Lupu, D. and R. Tiganasu. 2022. COVID-19 and the Efficiency of Health Systems in Europe. *Health Economics Review* 12(1).

MacGregor, H., M. Leach, G. Akello, L. Sao Babawo, M. Baluku, A. Desclaux, et al. 2022. Negotiating Intersecting Precarities: COVID-19, Pandemic Preparedness and Response in Africa. *Medical Anthropology* 41(1). 19–33.

Maddawin, A., P. Morgan, A. Park, D. Suryadarma, L. Trinh, and P. Vandenberg. 2024. Learning Disruptions during the COVID-19 Pandemic: Evidence from Household Surveys in Southeast Asia. *ADBI Working Paper*. Asian Development Bank Institute.

McKimm, A., N. Thomson, R. Vangucci, N. Huxley, and B. Coghlan. 2023. Meeting Summary: Improving Cross Agency Responses to Biological and Environmental Threats Across the Borders of the Greater Mekong Subregion. Bangkok.

Mobarak, A. M. 2023. Why Did COVID-19 Vaccinations Lag in Low- and Middle-Income Countries? Lessons from Descriptive and Experimental Data. *AEA Papers and Proceedings* 113. 637–641.

Molato-Gayares, R. and M. Thomas. 2022. Falling Further Behind: The Cost of COVID-19 School Closures by Gender and Wealth. *Asian Development Outlook 2022.* Asian Development Bank.

Moore, A. and P. Kortsaris. 2020. Adaptable Asylum Systems in Portugal in the Context of COVID-19. *Forced Migration Review* 65.

Moscoviz, L. and D. Evans. 2022. Learning Loss and Student Dropouts during the COVID-19 Pandemic: A Review of the Evidence Two Years after Schools Shut Down. *CGD Working Paper* 609. Center for Global Development.

Msemburi, W., A. Karlinsky, V. Knutson, S. Aleshin-Guendel, S. Chatterji, and J. Wakefield. 2023. The WHO Estimates of Excess Mortality Associated with the COVID-19 Pandemic. *Nature* 613. 130–137.

Narayanasamy, S., et al. 2023. Lessons from COVID-19 for Pandemic Preparedness: Proceedings from a Multistakeholder Think Tank. *Clinical Infectious Diseases* 77 (15 December). 1635–1643.

Nur Aisyah, D., A. F. Lokopessy, M. Naman, H. Diva, L. Manikam, W. Adisasmito, and Z. Kozlakidis. 2023. The Use of Digital Technology for COVID-19 Detection and Response Management in Indonesia: Mixed Methods Study. *Interactive Journal of Medical Research* 12. e41308.

OECD. 2021. Coronavirus (COVID-19) Vaccines for Developing Countries: An Equal Shot at Recovery (accessed 12 July 2023). Organisation for Economic Co-operation and Development.

Osewe, P. 2021. Pandemic Preparedness and Response Strategies: COVID-19 Lessons from the Republic of Korea, Thailand and Viet Nam. Asian Development Bank.

Our World in Data (OWID). 2023. Coronavirus (COVID-19) Vaccinations (accessed 12–13 July 2023).

Pappa, S., V. Ntella, T. Giannakas, V. G. Giannakoulis, E. Papoutsi, and P. Katsaounou. 2020. Prevalence of Depression, Anxiety, and Insomnia Among Healthcare Workers During the COVID-19 Pandemic: A Systematic Review and Meta-analysis. *Brain Behav Immun* 88. 901–907.

Robinson, A., A. Chang, J. Hammitt, and S. Resch. 2017. Understanding and Improving the One and Three Times GDP per Capita Cost-effectiveness Thresholds. *Health Policy and Planning* 32(1). 141–145.

Sachs, J. D., et al. 2022. The Lancet Commission on Lessons for the Future from the COVID-19 Pandemic. *The Lancet* 400(10359). 1224–1280.

Seale, H., C. E. F. Dyer, I. Abdi, K. M. Rahman, Y. Sun, M. O. Qureshi, A. Dowell-Day, J. Sward, and M. S. Islam. 2020. Improving the Impact of Non-pharmaceutical Interventions during COVID-19: Examining the Factors that Influence Engagement and the Impact on Individuals. *BMC Infectious Diseases* 20. 607.

Shadmi, E., et al. 2020. Health Equity and COVID-19: Global Perspectives. *International Journal for Equity in Health* 19(1).

Shin, J., S. Kim, and K. Koh. 2021. Economic Impact of Targeted Government Responses to COVID-19: Evidence from the Large-scale Clusters in Seoul. *Journal of Economic Behavior and Organization* 192. 199–221.

Stoto, M. A., A. Woolverton, J. Kraemer, P. Barlow, and M. Clarke. 2022. COVID-19 Data are Messy: Analytic Methods for Rigorous Impact Analyses with Imperfect Data. *Globalization and Health* 18(2).

Struelens, M. J. and P. Vineis. 2021. COVID-19 Research: Challenges to Interpret Numbers and Propose Solutions. *Frontiers in Public Health* 9. 651089.

Sumarto, S. 2016. The Art of Evidence-based Policy Making in Indonesian Social Policy. Presentation at the Knowledge Sector Initiative Workshop, 21 April. Jakarta.

Tanaka, S. 2022. Economic Impacts of SARS/MERS/ COVID-19 in Asian Countries. *Asian Economic Policy Review* 17(1). 41–61. Japan Center for Economic Research.

Vindegaard, N. and M. E. Benros. 2020. COVID-19 Pandemic and Mental Health Consequences: Systematic Review of the Current Evidence. *Brain, Behavior, and Immunity* 89. 531–542.

Wang, C. and H. Zhao. 2020. The Impact of COVID-19 on Anxiety in Chinese University Students. *Frontiers in Psychology* 11. 1168.

WHO. 2021. COVID-19 Strategic Preparedness and Response Plan Operational Planning Guideline.

———. 2023. Respiratory Pathogen Pandemic Preparedness: Lessons Identified from the Global Response to COVID-19. World Health Organization.

World Bank. 2022. World Development Report 2022: Finance for an Equitable Recovery. Chapter 1.

World Bank, UNESCO, UNICEF, UK-FCDO, USAID, and the Bill & Melinda Gates Foundation. 2022. The State of Global Learning Poverty: 2022 Update.

Wulandari, E. W., E. B. Hastuti, V. Setiawaty, V. Sitohang, and S. Ronoatmodjo. 2020. The First Intra-Action Review of Indonesia's Response to the COVID-19 Pandemic. *Health Security* 19(5). 521–531.

Xiong, J., O. Lipsitz, F. Nasri, L. M. W. Lui, H. Gill, L. Phan, D. Chen-Li, M. Iacobucci, A. Ho, R. Majeed, and R. S. McIntyre. 2020. Impact of COVID-19 Pandemic on Mental Health in the General Population: A Systematic Review. *Journal of Affective Disorders* 277. 55–64.

Yang, T. U., J. Y. Noh, J. Y. Song, H. J Cheong, and W. J. Kim. 2021. How Lessons Learned from the 2015 Middle East Respiratory Syndrome Outbreak Affected the Response to Coronavirus Disease 2019 in the Republic of Korea. *The Korean Journal of Internal Medicine* 36(2). 271–285.

Yoo, K. J., S. Kwon, Y. Choi, and D. M. Bishai. 2021. Systematic Assessment of South Korea's Capabilities to Control COVID-19. *Health Policy* 125(5). 568–576.